"Chris Furr's words are not for the faint of heart. Though not intentionally provocative, they will provoke you in the greatest sense nonetheless. His candor and conviction will challenge your assumptions, test the story you tell yourself, and galvanize you to live with more attention and intention. He reminds us that faith calls us to do the difficult but necessary work of confronting privilege both in the world and in the mirror."

—John Pavlovitz, author of *If God Is Love, Don't Be a Jerk*

"In *Straight White Male*, Chris Furr and contributors incisively and powerfully remind us that just because we didn't create the system doesn't mean we don't benefit from it. This call to straight, white men to recognize and deconstruct our privilege is both urgent and desperately needed. This book is a must-read!"

—Josh Scott, lead pastor, GracePointe Church, Nashville, Tennessee

"This graceful book offers a wise pastoral path toward the intentional deconstruction of straight, white, maleness, understood by author Chris Furr as a social construction that delivers privilege to some and harm to all and as fundamentally contrary to the gospel proclaimed and embodied by Jesus Christ. The book is deeply enriched by generous and illuminating contributions from Matthias Roberts, William J. Barber II, Melissa Florer-Bixler, and Robyn Henderson-Espinoza. Highly recommended."

—David P. Gushee, Distinguished University Professor of Christian Ethics, Mercer University

"From the start, *Straight White Male* gets right to the heart of the problems we face when we elevate patriarchal structures. Furr's use of Scripture and stories made his deconstruction (and reconstruction) personal and empowering."

—Brian Anderson, cofounder and executive director, Fathering Together

"*Straight White Male* couldn't come at a better time. With words permeated with humility and honesty, Chris Furr takes aim at the social forces plaguing American Christianity. If you are a straight, white dude like me, this thoughtful book needs to be in your hands. We need to read and absorb this book so that we can do better and seek the transformation Furr powerfully articulates in these pages."

—Billy Kilgore, writer, pastor, and stay-at-home dad

*Straight White Male*

# Straight White Male

## A Faith-Based Guide to Deconstructing Your Privilege and Living with Integrity

### CHRIS FURR

WESTMINSTER
JOHN KNOX PRESS
LOUISVILLE • KENTUCKY

*First edition*
Published by Westminster John Knox Press
Louisville, Kentucky

22 23 24 25 26 27 28 29 30 31—10 9 8 7 6 5 4 3 2 1

Unless otherwise indicated, Scripture quotations are from the New Revised Standard Version of the Bible, copyright © 1989 by the Division of Christian Education of the National Council of the Churches of Christ in the U.S.A., and are used by permission. Scripture quotations marked CEB are from the Common English Bible, © 2011 Common English Bible, and are used by permission.

*Book design by Drew Stevens*
*Cover design by Stephen Brayda*

**Library of Congress Cataloging-in-Publication Data**

Names: Furr, Chris, author.
Title: Straight white male : a faith-based guide to deconstructing your
    privilege and living with integrity / Chris Furr.
Description: First edition. | Louisville, Kentucky : Westminster John Knox
    Press, [2022] | Includes bibliographical references. | Summary:
    "Straight, white, male pastor Chris Furr offers a guide to
    deconstructing straight, white male privilege in conversation with
    William J. Barber II, Melissa Florer-Bixler, Robyn Henderson-Espinoza,
    and Matthias Roberts to provide a vision for how straight, white men can
    do better"-- Provided by publisher.
Identifiers: LCCN 2022003796 (print) | LCCN 2022003797 (ebook) | ISBN
    9780664266615 (paperback) | ISBN 9781646982493 (ebook)
Subjects: LCSH: Men, White--Religious life. | Heterosexual men--Religious
    life. | Christians, White--Religious life.
Classification: LCC BV4528.2 .F87 2022 (print) | LCC BV4528.2 (ebook) |
    DDC 248.8/42--dc23/eng/20220223
LC record available at https://lccn.loc.gov/2022003796
LC ebook record available at https://lccn.loc.gov/2022003797

Most Westminster John Knox Press books are available at special quantity discounts when purchased in bulk by corporations, organizations, and special-interest groups. For more information, please e-mail SpecialSales@wjkbooks.com.

*For Noah and Jude, with all my love*

*There's no such thing as someone else's war*
*Your creature comforts aren't the only thing worth fighting for.*
  —Jason Isbell and the 400 Unit, "White Man's World"

# Contents

# Introduction

This book is not about Donald Trump. I guess it's also not *not* about Donald Trump either, in that the world looked different to me the day after the 2016 election. Two profound things changed for me—the way I saw others, and the way I understood how others saw me. That may be only two things, but there aren't many bigger than that.

Of course, in the light of that Wednesday morning, it had not changed at all for the folks who were most threatened by a Trump presidency. America was as it had always been, a place hostile to people of color, a deeply patriarchal society standing on the foundation of white supremacy. Those who have not been able to afford to trust in America's better angels knew better and were not surprised. But it was an awakening for me, and I hope for others like me. We learned that we could no longer assume that the things we'd learned about in our history classes were, in fact, history. We learned that some of us held drastically different views of the world than others.

I am, by nature, a person who assumes the best about people, which leads me to make assumptions about people that I learned abruptly had not been true. That day, I found I was looking at people differently. Behind the counter at the sandwich shop where I bought my lunch, I examined the three white guys, roughly my age, wondering how they'd voted. They looked like me. They could be me. Had they preferred Trump? Had they ignored his misogynistic language and behavior? Heard and followed his racial dog whistles? Everywhere I looked, every person I saw, I wondered. The person driving the car next to me at the stoplight. The parents in the carpool line at my kids' school. The white guys on the daily podcast I loved, who dismissed the person of color on the show when he insisted that the results had not been about "economic anxiety" but about race. That was the last episode I ever downloaded.

My illusions had been shattered, I suppose, and the consequence was a silent interrogation of everyone around me, especially the ones who looked like me. I knew the demographics, that the overwhelming majority of college-educated straight white men had voted for Trump. It dawned on me (I will admit to not being the most perceptive person): if I was looking at everyone else this way, this was the way folks were likely looking at me. They could look at the car I drove, the color of my skin, the clothes I wore—even the job I do—and make certain assumptions about my political leanings, and therefore my values. I felt like an impostor in my own skin. I looked at people with whom I have so very much in common and instantly felt as though I was not familiar with them at all.

There is something mind-bending about fitting the appearance of a type, but being unable to understand or identify with the particular attributes that go along with that type, and why exactly it feels so foreign. In one sense, it was profoundly isolating to be walking around in a body that carried deep associations about who I am as a person, values with which I definitely did not want to be associated (again, "welcome," say millions of nonwhite, nonbinary others); to look and sound like one thing but feel internally like something else. It made me think deeply about how I want to be perceived, about how what I hold in my heart or mind isn't as important as where and how

I present my physical self to those around me, in ways that represent who I want to be. It was like one of those bad dreams about being in public with no clothes on. I was all of a sudden aware of what people saw when they looked at me. The election of Donald Trump was a catalyst for this, but this book is not about him, and the problem I hope to address did not begin with him and certainly will not end with him either. Straight white men have been the apex predators in our culture, and around the world, for centuries. We have wiped out Indigenous populations, owned people as property, used and abused the environment for profit, stigmatized both men and women for their sexual orientation or gender identity to destructive effect—all of this mostly, as I will show, as a means to soothe our own insecurities. This is why "predator" is an appropriate term—because we have made anyone and everyone the prey by which we have sustained ourselves. We may be socialized differently in the context of our communities, churches, parents and family, friends, education, and so on, but there is no escaping the broader context in which we all come up. We have been bred to dominate and consume. Deep down we, like most predators, still have an innate taste for those we can make our prey. We do not know who we are apart from this, or what we could be, if not predators.

However, it is possible for Jesus to ruin our appetite for dominance. Not just any Jesus. Not the one who has been co-opted in the name of justifying toxic masculinity, homophobia, economic oppression, and white supremacy. Not the one who was preached on plantations in the slaveholding South; neither the one conveniently cited by politicians, nor the benign Jesus offered in many mainline congregations by white male pastors, sentimentalized and explained away so as not to offend or demand. But the Jesus of the Gospels, the Jesus who disrupts social and economic systems bent on exploitation and inequality, the Jesus who casts a radical vision built not on consumption but on equity, the Jesus who critiques and questions religious practice that supports the status quo—*that* Jesus will spoil your appetite.

He spoiled mine in the summer of 2004, when I was a seminary intern following around the Rev. Dr. William J. Barber II and encountering a kind of salvation that could not be divorced from talking about bodies—about school districts and per pupil spending, affordable housing, and access to early childhood education. On the first day of my internship, the Rev. Barber asked me to meet him at the church in the early morning. I drove us around in his minivan. As we drove through various neighborhoods in Goldsboro, North Carolina, he told me about the demographics of those who lived in each neighborhood, what they had once been, where the children were districted to attend elementary, middle, and high school. We went to City Hall, where we asked for a large map that he had clearly consulted many times before. He spread it out over a large wooden conference table and talked to me about the geography of the place.

I had never considered this to be information that ministry might require—that following Jesus might require me to locate myself, bodily, in the midst of other bodies; to consider that how I sustained and enriched myself might deprive others. It was a new thing for me to consider that understanding how Title I funds are allocated, how schools qualify for them, and how they are used might be a matter of pastoral care to the congregation I serve.

In room after room we entered, often to have tense conversations with local leaders hostile toward him, I saw casual prejudice I had presumably been blind to previously. I learned to feel sorry for those who assumed that Barber's intellect did not match their own, because he was the most intelligent and learned person in whatever room we entered, and often that realization was painful and embarrassing for those who'd taken for granted that he was there to grandstand and had not done his homework (whether this was because of his race or because clergy do not generally possess deep knowledge of public policy, it is hard to say). Most of all, I encountered a Jesus I never knew.

Before that summer, I had an abiding faith: I believed in the power of Christian community; I believed that Jesus showed up and was present to the people of God in powerful ways, especially when they were serving one another. But I was swimming on the surface of a very deep ocean. I could've kept going just as I was, but I would've missed untold wonders (and dangers) underneath me. On Pentecost, Barber preached about the Holy Spirit—how the Spirit can be like a miner's light for us in dark and unfamiliar places, allowing us to see our surroundings as we never had before. He had a stack of pages on the pulpit but never made it much past page 2. I found myself no longer on the chancel behind the pulpit, but in front of the steps with many in the congregation, tears flowing down my cheeks—because the Spirit of God had done for me just what he described. I could see now, and what I had seen, I could not unsee.

Jesus ruined my appetite the semester that Dr. Peter Storey, who was president of the South African Council of Churches during the struggle against apartheid, introduced me to a Jesus who wasn't wrapped in the flag, but stood against and was executed by empire. Through the lens of his struggle with the apartheid government, Dr. Storey taught us what it looks like when elements of the church clothe themselves in white supremacy, in violence intended to maintain unjust order among God's people. This was, of course, right under my nose, in every American history course I'd ever taken, but the South African narrative helped me to see the narrative that had shaped me. He explained that America was the modern Rome, and that the rest of the world exists in the shadow of its empire. We watch your movies, listen to your music, and pay careful attention to your politics, because one way or another, they all find their way to us, he told us. "To be a responsible citizen in Rome," he said, in one of those moments where you remember where you were sitting, "you must know what it is like to live on the fringes of the empire."

That summer I served as a ministry intern in Pinetown, South Africa, just outside the city of Durban. On Saturdays I would walk to the mall and see hardly any other white faces. It was the first time I'd ever been conscious of myself as a minority. I did not want to be so ignorant of others' experience of the world any longer. I had been missing too much.

Jesus spoiled my appetite the day a gay woman in my congregation shared from the pulpit that our church was one of three places in the world she felt safe holding her spouse's hand. It was Laity Sunday, and instead of a sermon I asked three members of the congregation to share a Bible passage that had been important to them and why it was significant in their faith journey—a simple task. She chose a passage from the creation story: "So God created humankind in his image, in the image of God he created them" (Gen. 1:27). She talked about how long it had taken her to believe that those words were true about herself. She shared with us how unsafe she felt, generally, in the world, with a notable exception being the congregation I had been called to serve. I sat on the back row, weeping. I could not think of anything more important. I remembered Jesus calling the kin-dom of God a mustard bush, a place where "the birds of the air come and make nests in its branches" (Matt. 13:32), and pondered what it was like to find true sanctuary in the body of Christ. In that moment, I would not have cared if everyone else had left the church and if it were only me and those two women remaining. Even if that were the case, that was a hill on which I was willing to die—that a person should not live in fear because of the form that love takes in their life.

I do not want to belong to a church full of predators wearing Jesus like camouflage. I do not want my existence to be sustained by the suffering of another. This is what occurred to me driving around that day after the 2016 election. Jesus has made me a stranger among my own species. Even though I am surely guilty of operating as a predator, my heart's desire is not to do the harm men who look like me have done and are doing to the people who are nearest to the heart of Jesus. If I'm a predator—a lion—Jesus made me a vegetarian. I spent a lot of time exploring in my own head what it meant to discover that one's inner identity did not match what could be assumed from one's exterior. I think it was the first time I understood what people who look like me have been doing to everyone else for as long as anyone can remember.

That evening I sat at our dinner table with my wife, discussing how we had processed the day. She listened as I shared the vegetarian lion image, listened as I described this feeling of being unmoored and danced around the edges of feeling sorry for myself (bless her, she is patient). Finally, she looked at me and said, "Yes, but you still get to walk around the world like a lion." No matter what I feel about it, this identity shapes my existence. It comes with things I'd rather not accept, but it grants me privileges I cannot deny.

What does it mean to wear this identity in the world? What kind of life does this call me to live? What kind of parent, husband, friend, pastor, and disciple does this require me to be? It seems an insurmountable task to disentangle myself from a life in which almost everything I touch, from my iPhone to my groceries to my underwear, is the product of someone who is living poorly so that I do not. The alternative, however, is to march on, unmoved, unchallenged, shrugging my shoulders at what has gone before and accepting that the injustices I've inherited will be passed on to my children and theirs. While there are many problems with making that choice, the greatest problems are that it does not take the Jesus I have encountered seriously, and the Jesus I have encountered will not be taken anything but seriously.

Two things occurred to me in that moment. One is that it will never be possible for straight white men to be completely aware of our blindness to our own instincts—how we privilege our own point of view, assume that our voices should be heard and honored (or published), are ignorant of what our presence means to certain people in proximity to us. I cannot cure myself of this ignorance, and whatever ways I am able to unlearn these habits, I can only learn from those who are willing to tell me the truth, be Christ present to me. This is why, from the beginning, I knew that the pages of this book could not be filled only with my words. Inevitably I will speak out of turn, speak an incomplete truth or an outright falsehood, miss the way toward a redemptive way of living. Those who have offered their own words in the interest of our hearing the truth have offered us grace—words that folks like me are not owed, but are blessed by nonetheless, in the interest of our encountering the transformative grace of Christ.

The second realization I had that day at the dinner table was that men like me need a redemptive way to think about our identities. Learning the destructive legacy of white supremacy and patriarchy is a bit like learning that you have murderers in your family tree (I suppose many of us probably do). What does this mean about who we are? How do we carry this legacy in the world? How do we understand the people who raised us, the family members we loved and who loved us, who made us who we are, for better but also for worse? There is great grief to be encountered here, and too many of us are unwilling to face that reckoning because we do not know who we will be when the shedding of an old identity is underway. There is also guilt and shame, which are complex emotions that can be catalysts for lasting change in a person's life, but are by and large only obstacles if we cannot see a redemptive light at the end of that tunnel.

There are the conversations that justice-minded men are having in public, and then there are the ones they are having in private. In public, we acknowledge the struggles for justice all around us, from #MeToo to Black Lives Matter to LGBTQ+ rights. In private, people who look like me are wondering how to be themselves in this climate, what to do to still be fully ourselves while also acknowledging that people who look like us still have a grossly outsized amount of power and influence. I want to be clear that this is not an attempt to engender sympathy from those who have been harmed by straight white men for centuries, but deconstructing a particular worldview, which is surely required, leaves a raw and unformed possibility. It is in the best interest of everyone if straight white men find redemptive paths forward instead of retreating into destructive habits.

One possible outcome is that, faced with the challenge of departing from a particular identity, we begin to retreat even deeper into toxic expressions of this identity. One way of rejecting this hard work and the uncertainty that comes with it is to insist that the real problems are cancel culture, political correctness, and liberal politics. Among many other factors, Trumpism seems to be at least a partial response to attempts to redefine whiteness, maleness, straightness—if you say that I must change who I am, I will instead become an extreme version of that part of me which you believe is a problem. This temptation exists even for those not otherwise particularly inclined to extremism. Faced with a reckoning that requires hard work and points toward an unclear path, retreating is a very human response.

There has been much reckoning in our culture—many book clubs, Facebook groups, and organized protests. We have come face-to-face, once again, with the toxic legacy of patriarchy, and facing it is essential. To move beyond reckoning and toward redemption, however, we must begin to articulate a new vision for how we might carry ourselves in relation to others. "Redemptive" is an operative term; while stating the facts of whiteness and patriarchy has punitive elements that are meant to shock the conscience and appeal to our moral center, without a destination to pursue we are left only with shame, a toxic state of being that white men will surely weaponize rather than bearing it on their own. We are doing it now, in a new wave of hate speech and regressive politics.

I am aware that some will accuse me of a kind of self-hatred, will say that this entire project is rooted in a dissatisfaction with who I am that I've projected onto everyone else. Straight white men are notoriously aggressive when one of our own breaks rank. Even in informal conversations around patriarchy I have been called a "white knight" (one who comes to a woman's aid only to endear himself to her). Others seem to be puzzled with how much I think about race and how often it enters my teaching and preaching, but, as you may find, when you begin to see all the ways whiteness touches our life together, you can no longer ignore it; you see it everywhere you look.

I am no more at war with myself than Paul, who wrote to the church in Rome of his struggle to understand his own motivations, the way he carried himself in the world. Paul writes of a spiritual struggle that expresses itself in embodied ways: "I do not understand my own actions. For I do not do what I want, but I do the very thing I hate" (Rom. 7:15). Paul believes he has cultivated within himself the will to do what is right, the earnest desire to do what God calls us to do and be, but he finds that the rhythms and habits of his own life betray his will.

Much ink has been spilled over the distinction between flesh and spirit that Paul makes, but through an exploration of how these identities, worn and embodied in the world, have done historic harm, perhaps Paul's words come into clearer focus. With our hearts and minds we may desire to do and be different. We may have an intellectual grasp of the dynamics of race, sexuality, and gender. We may desire within ourselves to do no harm by our embodiments of these identities, but often we find that the habits and postures we have learned are not so easily broken. We do what we do not want to do, and fail to be what we are willing ourselves to be.

There is a certain peace in acknowledging this ongoing struggle and embracing it. As a child who grew up on the coast, I learned early on that too much fighting against an ocean current you are caught in can be a recipe for disaster—you will find quickly that you do not have the stamina. It is counterintuitive when you feel at risk, but sometimes choosing to breathe, relax your muscles, and embrace an uncomfortable and uncertain situation gives you the best chance to arrive in more peaceful waters with air still in your lungs. By the time most of us awaken to what it means to be white in a racialized society, or a man in a patriarchal culture that has narrowly defined masculinity, the work that must be done to unlearn the bad habits and poor postures we have developed is immense and may take the rest of our lives. The alternative, however, is perpetuating those things, passing them on to our children—and being another generation they read about in their history books and wonder why we lacked the courage and the commitment to face what was in front of us. My hope is that we can learn to relax and breathe and not fight so hard against the transformation we are being offered. Resisting change won't get us where we really want to go. To that end, I am more at peace with who I am now than I ever have been.

There are times when I wish I had not inherited the legacy that comes with my particular identity, yes; there are times when I hear or see a comment about patriarchy and feel the familiar "not all men" rebuttal rising up within me. Yet renewing my commitment to understanding, to discerning, to self-examination has allowed me to encounter the Spirit of God in new ways, to feel that Spirit resting on my head, lighting my surroundings, as the Rev. Barber said on that Pentecost Sunday. Now I feel that I am walking deeper and deeper into that cave, further along the path of discipleship. I have found a way of being that has meaning and purpose beyond me. I believe this is what Jesus meant when he said, "For those who want to save their life will lose it, and those who lose their life for my sake will find it" (Matt. 16:25). I am fine with losing the life I was given, because the one I continue to discover is richer and fuller. It is far from any kind of self-loathing. It feels more like loving myself so that I am more capable of loving my neighbor.

To begin, we must name where we are and practice the oft-avoided Christian practice of confession. In my ministry, I frequently have been surprised by the power that simple acknowledgment of past harm can have. There is nothing particularly remarkable about acknowledging the facts of history, though we have had trouble doing this and still do. I have been reminded of its power by the responses I often receive, something like: "I've never heard someone who looks like you acknowledge what you just did." Again, this is not a particular virtue, but it does have restorative power when it comes to our relationships with those who do not share our particular identity. It signals a departure from the legacy of gaslighting we have perpetrated on those around us, who have experienced one reality while we have operated as if another one exists entirely. What a relief it must be to hear the truth of your existence acknowledged by those who have worked so hard to define (and often diminish) it. This, alone, for the healing power it carries for those whose lives have been unnecessarily made more difficult simply because of who they are, is worth the challenge of truth-telling.

Additionally, there is no way forward without having the courage to tell ourselves the truth. We cannot be so interested in self-preservation that we would rather live a lie than embrace the call of God to work for love and justice—not if we want to call ourselves disciples of Jesus. For that reason, we acknowledge at least a portion of how the lived realities of whiteness, masculinity, and heteronormativity have been harmful, both to others and to ourselves. This will be woefully incomplete—doubtless many will find unacknowledged history or this confession incomplete, but it is meant to be a beginning, not an ending.

This book is also intended to be a guide to deconstructing a particular worldview and reconstructing a new one—to help develop a distaste for that which harms others and ourselves, in favor of a more redemptive way of being present in the world. In the church, we sometimes call it conversion. Few are converted, however, without an encounter with the liberating power of Christ. For some, like the blind man at Bethsaida or the paralyzed man lowered through the roof by his friends, their transformative encounters with Christ are restorative; where once they were isolated from community, the bodily healing that Christ offers restores them to their place of belonging. For others—the rich man who wants to inherit eternal life, Nicodemus, and Zacchaeus, to name a few—Jesus complicates their lives and becoming his disciple will cost them. What you read in the pages that follow may be one or the other for you, but prayerfully both. There is a life to be gained from shedding the life we have inherited via toxic patterns that have oppressed and dehumanized others. I want to keep walking toward it, to be a predator who has learned other ways to sustain himself besides the same old hunting. And I want to help others come with me. My prayer is that you will come along.

# 1
## *The Lie Beneath*

I suppose it started with cell phone cameras. We who call ourselves white had been pretty convinced that lynching stopped with Jim Crow, that the civil rights movement had awakened white Americans to the common humanity possessed by people of every hue and had more or less made racism in America a thing of the past. But then we opened our social media accounts and watched Tamir Rice get shot for playing in the park with a toy gun and Eric Garner trying to breathe and George Floyd calling for his mother. In many ways, we'd lived in a different world—a world where the election of a Black president made a statement about the progress we'd made, and the long-standing problems of our past could be put to rest—but those videos pierced the veil, made us all realize that there isn't one world but many. There's the world white folks live in, where those who get in trouble with the police must have done something wrong, and then there is the one where people of color are still getting stopped by police in obscenely disproportionate numbers, still getting passed over for jobs, still not getting equal education, still dying. The cell phone cameras that recorded those moments helped those worlds collide.

Along the way, the #MeToo movement emerged, and the parallel world women live in was revealed to us as well. One by one, Hollywood actors, producers, musicians, and thinkers who shaped us were revealed to be sexual predators, and we were left to wonder if we should confess a different kind of "me too." Have I made a suggestive comment that left someone feeling harassed? Did the physical encounters I've had with women—from hugs to the much more intimate—take place with consent and without coercion? Have I talked down to a woman because I assumed what we were talking about was beyond her knowledge? These are challenging questions some of us were willing to ask ourselves, while others immediately feared something we'd said or done might be "misconstrued" and bring disproportionate consequences for behavior we'd never thought of as problematic. Once again, the revelation was that women's experience of the world was profoundly different from what we imagined (if we had even given it much thought).

Social media allowed for widespread connection between women and provided a platform for these stories to be told, in much the same way recordings of racialized violence had placed that reality in front of our eyes. The pain and trauma those stories contained and the sheer number of them made the moment a reckoning that could not be ignored. All of a sudden, we realized that sexual assault and harassment are an epidemic, and that the statistics mean that either we or someone we know well has been involved in one or the other or both. What we thought was normal wasn't anymore, because it never was—not to anyone other than straight white men.

This cultural moment represents an opportunity for those who have felt the deep pain and loss from generations of straight white men who have used them to hold power, feel dominant, and acquire wealth. It is a chance to seize on the momentary awareness of those who hold power, those who are awakening to the idea that so much of how we have defined who we are and gained what we have is rooted in the suffering of others. In this moment of awareness, when we are beginning to see what we had been blind to before, it is possible for us to be partners with those who have cried out for breath or worked to summon the courage to say "me too." That possibility only exists, however, if we are able and willing to see what we had not seen before, to accept and acknowledge our responsibility for the creation of unjust systems that have led to vastly different experiences of being human, and to accept that making these unjust, parallel worlds into one where all of God's children can be free to be as God created them involves us.

## OPEN YOUR EYES

While the cell phone cameras and the hashtags were a catalyst for some of us, the lived experience of people of color, women, and the LGBTQ+ community have always been in plain sight, were we inclined to see them. There is a lot at stake in seeing, however. If I see injustice and inequality, and I see that it is within my power to address it, I must make a choice. That choice may demand things of me, things I would rather not have to give, so it is better for me not to see at all.

Many of us have been at stoplights where a person stands, cardboard sign in hand, asking for whatever we might be able to give, however small. Only a pane of glass separates us, and there is nothing to stop our eyes from meeting theirs. If my gaze turns from the car in front of me, and I make eye contact with the person next to me, I have seen—I have seen their need, I have seen their asking, I have seen their humanity, and something within me changes. If my conscience is swayed, perhaps I reach for whatever coins or small bills are in my pockets. If I have nothing to give, I may give a knowing and sympathetic glance. But once I have seen, I am involved. To see but ignore is to refuse compassion.

Sometimes I imagine that this person is Jesus, in the same way he told us in Matthew 25 he would be found among the hungry, the thirsty, the sick or imprisoned. I know what discipleship requires of me if I see, if I see Jesus there. If I refuse this person in their need, then I refuse Jesus himself. When he told that story, Jesus said there would be people who would claim not to have seen his need—"'Lord, when was it that we saw you hungry or thirsty or a stranger or naked or sick or in prison, and did not take care of you?'" (v. 44). If only they had seen, they would have done something. There is a lot at stake in seeing. Some days I look. Some days I stare straight ahead and pray for the light to change.

Straight white men have done a lot of staring straight ahead, waiting for the light to change. The lies we tell ourselves are ways of not seeing: "He'll probably just spend it on alcohol" or "Why doesn't he get a job?" Similarly, we say, "He should've complied with the officer's orders." "She was asking for it." "Marriage equality redefines marriage." None of these things are true, but they help us drive past inequality, violence, and oppression without feeling obligated to stop, without having to change anything about our own lives or give up any of the power or privilege we have acquired in order to make things right. As the need in front of us becomes more difficult to ignore, we retreat deeper into the lies we tell ourselves.

For many straight white men, the lies we tell ourselves become hardened political beliefs meant to push back against the notion that these struggles for equality and liberation are worth engaging. Black Lives Matter, then, can be labeled a kind of exceptionalism, rebutted with "All Lives Matter," instead of being heard as the cry for equality and the recognition of our common humanity that it is. We should ask ourselves if this is an actual way of seeing the world or simply a defense mechanism, constructed (consciously or unconsciously) to spare us the reckoning that comes with acknowledging that historically, and in far too many places today, Black lives have not mattered the way that all human lives should. This is one of the paths in front of us, one that we could take when given the opportunity to see the world as it is, when people whose lives have been dramatically impacted by the way we have led ours are demanding that we see them. Many of us have taken this path, the one that affords us blindness, and will continue to do so.

There is privilege in having a choice at all and in choosing not to see. In the flood of body camera footage and videos taken by bystanders, I have grown weary of seeing people plead for their lives, their faces animated with fear; of hearing the pop of gunfire and seeing the way the human body reacts to the impact of a bullet. There is trauma in those images, and there is certainly danger in continuing to view images of Black death as a form of voyeurism. Still, I have a choice to watch or not. If I do not watch, then I can be spared the nausea and anger that come with seeing those images over and over, realizing that each one is someone's father, brother, sister, daughter. This is privilege—I can choose to see this violence or not, choose to let it change the course of my day or week or month, or not. Because my skin is white, these images will not be on my mind when my child leaves the house or when I see blue lights flashing in my rearview mirror. I do not have to hold this trauma in my body, do not have to worry about being followed around a store or viewed as a threat while out jogging, about living with what it means to constantly be viewed as a threat simply for existing.

Because I am not LGBTQ+, I do not have to wonder if the church I visit will accept me, if my neighbors will welcome me or ostracize me. I am free from persistently wondering if who I am will be met with painful rejection. Because I am not a woman, I grab whatever I feel like wearing out of my closet, without a thought for what parts of my body it will reveal and how others will interpret that. I can walk through the world without feeling that someone's eyes are on me.

Acknowledging privilege is difficult because if I do, I admit to possessing an advantage I did not earn. The anger and defensiveness I have seen in the faces of men at the suggestion that being a man carries with it advantages that we did not earn is remarkable. In America, hard work and upward mobility are central to the myth that defines our culture. If I have a lot, it's because I worked hard for it. If someone else has more than I do, they must have played the game better than I did, and I can't begrudge them for it. To suggest that I did not earn what I have but had it given to me (at least in part) exposes the great

American myth in which I have placed so much faith and brings me again to a choice. If I am in possession of stolen goods—an advantage, a fortune, the benefit of the doubt, all the ways in which it pays in America to be a straight white male—then I must choose whether I will keep what is not rightfully mine or give it back. It would be better for me if there were no such thing as privilege in the first place, which is perhaps why the word itself gives us such visceral reactions. If I open my eyes and see it for what it is, then I am accountable for what I do next.

As you will see in the essays contributed by my four esteemed coauthors, many people without the privilege trifecta of cisgender-heterosexual white males have privilege in some circles. A gay white man benefits from race and gender privilege that a Black trans woman does not. An educated LGBTQ+ person of color enjoys advantages from having received opportunities others may not have. A Black woman whose family could pay for her education may enjoy financial privilege that women saddled with student loans do not. A person with a high metabolism enjoys privilege that a person who struggles with obesity does not. The contributors to this book will help us think about where different kinds of privilege manifest themselves in our life together.

It is up to us what we do when we have an opportunity to address privilege, to deconstruct the reality that these traits grant us power over others. The next step after seeing is acknowledging—for ourselves and for our neighbors—the imbalance of power between us that allows some to flourish while others struggle.

## TELL THE TRUTH

Once I began a sermon with a series of questions. I asked people how they would respond if I said that they were sinners. Almost uniformly, having felt the need to be in a church on a Sunday morning, they shrugged their shoulders and nodded that they would agree to that statement without much trouble. Next,

I asked them how they would feel if I asked them to be specific about their sins. Would you treat it like a job interview, I asked them, and try to turn your worst traits into qualifications? ("It's hard for me to find Sabbath time with all the work I'm doing at the food pantry on the weekends.") Or acknowledge generic things like materialism, being judgmental or envious, losing your temper? Still everyone was sitting comfortably in their chairs, perhaps assured by the fact that in mainline Protestantism, everyone knows we long ago abandoned the practice of being specific in our confessions with anyone but God, and then only in emergencies. But then I asked how they would respond if I said that one of their sins is racism. Immediately the air left the room and I got awkward stares looking back at me.

Even after thinly veiled racist rhetoric has surged back into the mainstream over the past few years, the overwhelming majority of people recoil at the thought of being labeled in this way, because of its social unacceptability and moral implications. Even the most thinly veiled rhetoric comes with a denial of the white supremacy or patriarchy it so clearly conveys; those who implement racist immigration policy or misogynistic health care policy deny those labels because there is at least some public relations cost to seeing them attached. But if you're white, you are a participant in racist systems. If you're a man, the patriarchy is down deep in your core. It need not be that we are actively nurturing and sharing racial prejudice, such as knowingly using racist language. Each of us has been acculturated in a racialized way, meaning we have observed— subconsciously, even if we intellectually deny these things— that skin color matters and that there is power in whiteness.

I benefit from my whiteness in ways that I may intellectually find problematic but am not prepared to actually address in my way of life. This means I participate in racist systems, knowingly and unknowingly. Likewise, patriarchy shapes everything around us—our economic, social, and religious life—as women are denied certain opportunities and make eighty-two cents for every dollar earned by a man.[1] I belong to that world, and so do you. I carry implicit bias that I have absorbed my

entire life that will take the rest of my life to try and unlearn. It
is part of the sin we carry.

The way forward from this place, however, is not denial
or defensiveness. We see, and then we describe what we see.
The way forward starts with acknowledgment: confession.
To refuse confession is to hold a spiritual sickness within and
decline treatment.

It is necessary to pay attention to the bodily responses that
rise up as, in the chapters to come, portions of our collective
sins are outlined. It is natural to be defensive and anxious, to
reach for excuses or deflections; in fact, the perpetuation of
those very systems depends on those reactions, which is why
we are still here as a culture and as a church discussing the same
issues that our parents and grandparents faced. It's time that
we not only open our eyes but also confess what we see. There
are so many around us who have waited for straight white men
to own the truth of their own lives, and that many more who
are sure we will never do it.

If we call ourselves Christians, we must be prepared to be
exposed to the parts of ourselves that are not congruent with
the way of Jesus. This happens several times in the Gospels:
Jesus encounters someone who says with their words that they
want to follow him but, inevitably, Jesus names the very thing
with which they are not willing to part and asks them to give
it up. The rich man goes away grieving (Mark 10:22). One
wants to go and say goodbye to those at his home before he
sets out with Jesus, and Jesus says, "No one who puts a hand
to the plow and looks back is fit for the kingdom of God"
(Luke 9:62). Jesus is open with his disciples that the demands
of building their lives around him could cost them relationships, even with those most important to them; he came, he
said, not to bring peace but a sword (Matt. 10:34–39), to so
transform the lives of his followers that it may bring division
even in the areas of their lives they hold dearest.

We may ask ourselves, what is it that I am not willing to
compromise for my discipleship? That question may yield a
variety of answers. If pride, privilege, wealth, or power are

among them, then we place limits on our experience of the life
Christ offers us.


## BEYOND INDIVIDUAL SIN

In his classic book *Jesus and the Disinherited*, theologian Howard Thurman argues that the predominant voice of Christianity has evolved to speak primarily to the powerful. The book
was first published in 1949, and since then not much has
changed about the prevailing voice of Christianity. On display
in multicampus megachurches, in old clapboard churches in
one-stoplight towns, and in much of mainline Protestantism is
a brand of Christianity that focuses on individual salvation and
personal morality, suggesting that God cares more about our
being optimistic or nice or prosperous than about bringing a
more just, loving, and peaceable world into being. To empha-
size only our personal piety fails to take into account the whole
of the biblical narrative, in which God liberated the Hebrew
people from bondage, decried the abuse of the marginalized by
the powerful both in and outside the religious community, and
was embodied in a poor Palestinian Jew named Jesus of Nazareth. More specifically, it risks minimizing the ways in which
God—often through human actors—works to bring down systems that exploit the vulnerable in order to create and maintain
wealth and security for a few.

This need not be personal for you in order for you to be
accountable for it, which is among the most difficult things
for straight white men to accept. It is not necessary for us to
have built the system in order to benefit from it. All that anti-
LGBTQ+ bias needs to survive—once it is ingrained in the
culture—is for those who are not directly affected by it, or feel
we don't hold the bias ourselves, to abdicate any opportunity
we may have to challenge the patterns of exclusion that harm
our LGBTQ+ siblings. We would like to think that personal
responsibility—another central American ideal—would excuse
us from cleaning up the mess that someone else made or healing

the harm that someone else did, but it simply doesn't work that way, because our lives are too intertwined. "My ancestors didn't own slaves" and "Not all men . . ." are the refrains we turn to when we find ourselves resenting this reality and turning to defensiveness. Passing over a résumé because it bears the name of someone we believe is Black or discouraging our kids from playing with the girl on the playground who has two dads are the sins we commit as individuals, and with enough work on our own hearts and minds we can begin to leave them behind. However, the larger sins matter just as much—the norms that create such pressure in the mind of a trans teen that they contemplate suicide, the craftily drawn district lines that isolate racial groups in particular schools, a justice system that adds to the difficulty of sexual assault survivors reporting crimes perpetrated against them—and these take all of us to undo, whether we believe ourselves personally guilty or not.

In Scripture, God often intervenes on behalf of the disinherited, those made vulnerable by the structures established for power, wealth, and security. They are widows and orphans, made vulnerable by patriarchy; foreigners, made vulnerable by ethnic enmity; the poor, those whose labor is exploited to enrich those who already possess more than they need. God intends to disrupt the structures that sustain this status quo. Consider Mary's song, which many of us read in each Advent season without realizing that she is talking about us:

> "[God] has shown strength with his arm;
>      he has scattered the proud in the thoughts of their hearts.
> He has brought down the powerful from their thrones,
>      and lifted up the lowly;
> he has filled the hungry with good things,
>      and sent the rich away empty."
>
>                                        (Luke 1:51–53)

These words are spoken in the past tense; what Mary describes has already happened, by virtue of the baby in her belly, Jesus. The task, then, for those who find themselves with power, with wealth, with privilege, is to discern what it would mean for us to accept this Jesus as the savior of our lives. This is difficult work that should not be minimized.

## PULL IT UP BY THE ROOT

"Deconstruction" is an increasingly popular word, as those who were raised in particular brands of Christianity that they have found to be harmful are engaging in the lengthy, emotionally taxing practice of taking down the belief system and resulting identity that was created for them, in order that they may build back a faith that might be reconciled with who they have discovered God to be and who they found themselves to be, as human beings created in the image of God.

As I write this, one of the lingering home improvement projects that has gone undone is replacing all the boards on our back deck. Over the past few years, as individual boards have rotted, I have replaced them. But there are places where the boards are buckling because of the support beams underneath, and places where the previous installer screwed them down too close together, so that rain does not drain properly and pools on the surface instead. To really fix it, all the boards need to be taken up, the underlying problems addressed, and a new deck installed. Fixing it piece by piece is a temporary fix, not a solution. The same applies to our discipleship. Sometimes it is necessary to undergo a deconstruction, so that you can build back something that will last.

We have done too little of this discernment. The faith handed down to many of us reinforces our own position in a culture where there is so much injustice and so much suffering, rather than sounding the clarion call of a poor Palestinian Jew (and his mother, among others in the biblical narrative) to examine our social location and our complicity in systems that perpetuate the status quo that runs wildly counter to the priorities of Jesus we find in the Gospels.

This support for the status quo takes place in both active and passive ways. Actively, we have seen Jesus associated with a forceful brand of masculinity, which even those with casual knowledge of the Jesus in the Gospels can identify as a falsehood. Many of us at least have feelings of unease at overt displays of Christian nationalism, where the name of Jesus is invoked as bombs are dropped, or elected officials are portrayed as God's elect. These are easily identifiable contradictions, from which those who wish to stay comfortably "in the middle" can steer clear. To define discipleship as a life of benevolence, of generosity that also fits within a life of accumulation—of resources, of advantage—is perhaps a greater danger, because it leads many of us to participate in a pattern of Christian life that does little to change anything about structures that perpetuate inequality and injustice. We are replacing rotting deck boards on the surface, in other words.

"This is a matter of tremendous significance," Thurman writes, "for it reveals to what extent a religion that was born of a people acquainted with persecution and suffering has become the cornerstone of a civilization and of nations whose very position in modern life has too often been secured by a ruthless use of power applied to weak and defenseless peoples."[2] Thurman is onto an inherent contradiction in the theology and ecclesiology formed by generations of straight white men: Jesus was not one of us and did not come, particularly, to minister to us. On the contrary, we find ourselves at the top of the hierarchies Jesus was interested in dismantling. We resent the Pharisees along with Jesus, but we are more often religious people who have resigned ourselves to working within the status quo. We see the Roman Empire through the eyes of first-century Jews like Jesus but fail to see the inherent conflict in belonging among a majority that wields outsized power here (and around the world). Jesus rebukes the religious slut-shamers who are ready to stone a woman to death; he draws in Samaritans and Gentiles, challenging the identity politics of his own people.

We see ourselves in the heroes of the story, but an honest look at the Gospel narrative calls that into question. Rather than telling the truth about who we are most like in the story, we have ignored what we could, explained away what we couldn't, and flat-out lied about the rest. The intellectual gymnastics it takes to read the Gospels without finding serious contradiction to our lives are quite impressive. We have knocked all the sharp edges off of Jesus until he fits nicely into the confines of whiteness, patriarchy, and heteronormativity.

The Spirit, however, is not so easily contained. The Spirit of God disrupts, disturbs, challenges, and convicts in the interest of transformation and salvation. Christian communities that challenge the norms, that look more like the cast of discarded people Jesus gathered to himself, are taking on vitality that many churches filled with modern-day Pharisees lack. House for All Sinners and Saints, founded by Nadia Bolz-Weber in Denver, Colorado, and Galileo Church in Fort Worth, Texas, founded by Katie Hays, are two examples among many. These communities, including queer folk from the beginning and with women in leadership, have begun to draw people away from established communities that have operated as if the boundaries of God's family are settled. Something different happens when the neatly formed boundaries that exclude and demean come down; the Spirit is on the move.

God is intent on expanding the love and justice that define the kin-dom of God that Jesus came to bring, and the Spirit is the agent of transformation, inviting human beings to be cocreators with God in a radical reordering of the world. We might expect disruption, challenge, and discomfort along the way, as the Spirit works within each of us and calls us to new lives and new vocations we might never have imagined. This is what we find over and over again in Scripture. If the version of the Christian life we are being offered is one that more or less allows our lives to remain the same, with only a few internal, spiritual improvements and a donation every now and then, we should be suspicious.

## WHAT DOES THE LORD REQUIRE OF YOU?

For straight white men, trying to be disciples of Jesus by practicing charity without accepting that we must dismantle the racist, patriarchal structures upon which we stand leads to further brokenness. Many of us have learned that discipleship requires that we respond to those in need with benevolence, and we share out of the abundance of what we have. Often, this looks like food pantries and homeless shelters, mission trips and domestic-violence ministries. There is much in the ministry of Jesus that not only encourages but requires that we give to those who need; indeed, Jesus tells us that when we minister to those who are hungry or thirsty or naked or in prison, we minister to him. The urgency of triage when it comes to our ministry to those in need should not be diminished—women suffering domestic abuse and homeless LGBTQ+ teens need a safe place to be in the moment—but it is theological malpractice to keep pulling babies out of the river and never go upstream to figure out who is putting them in and why.

Most churchgoers belong to a congregation that is committed to addressing the immediate needs in its community. Far fewer belong to one committed to addressing the larger systemic problems that create those needs, because these conversations often lead to conflict that may hurt church attendance or, worse, diminish the donor pool; or, because we are simply conflict averse in many mainline churches, we avoid conversations around systemic injustice because of how closely they have become aligned with partisan politics. We busy ourselves with many things—sometimes worthwhile things—that obscure the larger deconstruction we must do, within ourselves and within the Christian communities to which we belong.

When this is our sole way of practicing the call of Jesus to minister to those whose lives are continually undone by straight, white, cisgender norms, it places those with power (and the wealth that often comes with it) at the top of a paternalistic structure, sometimes unwittingly. It allows us to fit Jesus' call to address issues of poverty and oppression into our lives as they are, by continually treating symptoms rather than the disease itself. This demands little in the way of transformation, and often sustains power dynamics and privilege rather than creating systems of justice. As we will see, "benevolence" has been used to justify colonization as evangelism, slavery as salvation, and misogyny as protection. We think we are doing good—indeed, what Jesus asks of us—but the good it mostly does is to serve as an anesthesia to the deeper issues right in front of us. We inevitably respond to those seeking their humanity with derision, because they will not accept the incremental charity we are willing to give them. Even the most progressive among us wander toward these thoughts and attitudes. It is a symptom of a Christian ethic of service that does not question the dynamics of power and why they exist. Not only are those patterns dehumanizing to those who suffer because of them, but they are stumbling blocks in our relationships with our neighbors and, by extension, our relationship with God.

Eventually, perpetually existing in a state where one *has* and another *needs* alters the way we see one another as human beings. We develop disdain for those who are always in need of some concession from someone who has what we do—money, power, or influence. Yet it is also true that we are largely not interested in relinquishing those things so that there may no longer be a need for constant asking and giving.

The resulting irony is that we are hostile to those asking for relief from the structures created to work against them, as if they have a choice or preference. I dare say no one who has served in any of the ministries named above has been free from this kind of disdain: the person loading food from the food pantry has a nicer car than they should have, that woman calls the church office too regularly for assistance paying her bills. It is a short distance to travel from here to the belief that poverty is a result of poor choices, that the effects of institutional racism have long since run their course, that women should simply be smarter about how they dress or where they walk at night. This is easily observed in the forceful backlash in response to the #MeToo movement, for example, or conversations around nonbinary gender identity. Women who, for centuries, have had little to no recourse when it comes to sexual violence committed by men reach for agency, for a voice, and men respond with fear about false accusations. Nonbinary siblings of ours, created in the image of God, are now freer to claim a gender identity that does not fit the traditional fixed, binary choices, and we learn of the great emotional and spiritual toll this lack of freedom has had. In response, white men pass regressive legislation to address nonexistent problems with bathroom usage. Every time these laws are passed, suicide hotlines report a spike in calls. And yet, the white men who are frequently behind these laws point to belief in God as a motivation. In reality, the animosity defies explanation, apart from the fact that we have somehow gotten tired of being asked to make even incremental changes so that others might live, in a very real sense. This is wholly incongruent with following a Jesus who told us that no one has greater love than the one who lays down their life for a friend.

We serve a Savior who modeled what it means to empty one's self of one's privilege in the interest of others being liberated. Paul urges the Christians at Philippi to have the same mind that was in Christ Jesus,

> who, though he was in the form of God,
>     did not regard equality with God
>     as something to be exploited,
> but emptied himself,
>     taking the form of a slave,
>     being born in human likeness.
> And being found in human form,
>     he humbled himself
>     and became obedient to the point of death—
>     even death on a cross."
>                                (Phil. 2:6–8)

When the dynamics of our relationships with others lead to resentment rather than greater compassion, it is time to tell the truth about what is happening and search for the transformational power of God's Spirit, so that we might love our neighbors as ourselves.

## KEEP GOING

The prophet Jonah is an interesting biblical study in how we process resistance and defensiveness and find ways to keep going. He was called to a ministry he knew would expose aspects of God's character that would upset the way Jonah preferred to see things. When Jonah witnesses the dramatic repentance of the Ninevites, and God changes God's mind about the destruction God had promised, Jonah says, in essence, "I knew it, and this is precisely why I wanted no part of this." The end of the story finds Jonah outside of town, pouting and sulking that God had done what Jonah knew God would do—be as merciful to Jonah's enemies as God was to Jonah, and demonstrate that the justice and mercy of God was for them as well.

All of us construct a framework for understanding how the world works, how God works, and resist challenges to it because of the uncertainty and chaos it might bring to our lives, as Jonah did. The fear is that beginning to question what we have always considered an absolute will be like pulling the thread on a sweater—if you keep pulling, the whole thing will come apart. We are not sure that there is life on the other side of deconstruction, or if it is possible to rebuild a life that allows us to value our ancestors even if they made terrible and immoral choices, or to have a redemptive view of ourselves even if we acknowledge that those who look like us have wreaked terrible havoc on the world. The result, however, is a life lived hiding from truth, from a broader experience of the world.

If I resist the notion that I come from a country built on violence against Black and Brown bodies and the abuse of the land, I can maintain a certain identity like my father and my father's father and his father before him, and like many of my peers, who hold onto pride but cut themselves off from the sacred image of God in the humans around them, especially those whose suffering has paid for our privilege. How do we keep going when the opportunity to engage these truths feels as if it might open up the ground on which we stand?

Following Jesus means leaving an old identity behind, despite what you may have heard about just being the best version of the person you already are. To repent is to stop going in one direction, to turn around. This is different from what you might've learned about what it means to repent. To repent is not just to feel sorry about or guilty for the things you've done wrong, and promise to do better. It is deeper and more profound and more connected to other people than that. To repent is to make a lifestyle change, to fundamentally change the way you live and the way you relate to those around you, and—and this is a big piece of it—to change the way you participate in the systems that make the world go.

Over and over, the demands Jesus makes of those who would follow him require this kind of reordering. The disciples leave behind their vocations and the life that accompanied them; the rich young man is told that the next step, after keeping the basic commandment to love God and neighbor, is to sell everything he has and give the money to the poor. He goes away grieving. Another person wants to go and bury his father before he leaves to follow Jesus, and Jesus tells him that no one who puts hand to the plow and looks back is worthy of the kin-dom of God. Discipleship is not casual, not sentimental. It is about the transformation of one's mind but also about the embodiment of that transformation. There is always a reckoning that precipitates that kind of change—a moment to face the most significant impediment within ourselves to our being transformed by love of God in Christ.

Jesus had—and, I suppose, has—a way of reaching directly for that with which we are least willing to part. But to fear the kind of reckoning that might come with discovering how your place in the world may impede the justice that characterizes God's kin-dom and the reordering of your life that follows is to fear the salvation offered in Christ Jesus himself.

This is what it means to be specific when we confess that we have not loved our neighbors as ourselves; to do so is to be as moved by another's desire for freedom as we are driven by our own obsession with security. What is there to take seriously about a Jesus who has nothing to say to parents of Black and Brown children who must give instructions to their children on how best to return home safely? Or to women who must always be conscious, in stairwells and on sidewalks and in boardrooms, of who is in proximity to them and what they may desire? Or to a trans youth who contemplates self-harm each time it is reinforced that the church to which they belong finds their identity to be a falsehood? Moreover, what does Jesus have to say to those of us who carry none of these same fears or anxieties in our daily lives, who are free to worship and write and talk about Jesus of Nazareth in terms of a future life, because we can take for granted the life we have now?

The questions for those of us who do not live with fear, poverty, or violence because of our race, gender, or sexuality are whether or not we find it in contradiction to our discipleship that others do live with these threats, and whether or not we will continue to ignore the Jesus who has plenty to say to us as well. To begin, we must be moved by those for whom the establishment of this identity we possess has been immeasurably costly. It is fearful to think that we have grown so callous to the struggles of our neighbors, or so protective of our own place, that we can no longer be "moved with compassion" as Jesus frequently was by those around him.

By nature, wrestling with these questions leads to unpleasant confrontations within our own lives as we examine our own place in those systems and the ways our lifestyles themselves contribute to them, both actively and passively. The exploration of issues of race, gender, and sexuality in this book is an attempt to create that kind of confrontation within those of us whose race, gender, or sexuality is positioned at the top of those systems.

In the pages that follow, there are two chapters each on three defining identities: straight, white, and male. To begin, I will describe how the construction of these classifications has been harmful to others and to those who claim them. Each of these chapters will be followed by a second that offers redemptive ways of carrying these labels in the world, and words from a contributor who lives on the other side of being straight, white, or male—or all three.

Deconstruction is hard work. This is why, at the outset of this chapter, you were invited to take stock of the different emotions that arise within you as you read. Our brains will work behind the scenes to create the conditions that allow us to retreat into well-established patterns of thinking and behaving. It is easy to think that change is detrimental, but God invites us to go beyond a surface-level view of what change means, for our lives and for the world.

Among the great lies of white supremacy and patriarchy is the notion that they are so beneficial to white men that we do not want to live without them. The truth, however, is that while they have provided immense material benefit, they have also been an ongoing spiritual death. Slowly, daily, we are breathing in the toxic fumes of these things and believing they are life-giving when, in reality, they take us further and further from our neighbors and therefore further and further from God.

The hard work of deconstructing these beliefs and habits within us, and in our wider culture, will be worth doing only if you believe that the way of discipleship, though costly, is the way to life; if you believe Jesus when he says that the way to hold onto this life is to let go of it, that the way to find one's self is to lose the self you have and discover who Christ is calling you to be.

And so we begin with confession, by telling the truth. James Baldwin famously said that "not everything we face can be changed, but nothing can be changed until it is faced."[3] The dismantling of these systems in ways that most allow for healthier, redemptive patterns of living will involve straight white men. It is not necessary for us to comply in order for these toxic realities to crumble; this much we know, in the same way Pharaoh finally came to know that his will for the Israelites was not ultimately decisive. But the kin-dom of God that Jesus came to bring us includes forgiveness for the predator, the one we are sure is beyond redemption, the betrayer.

When I am sure that person cannot be me, I am troubled; when I accept that it is me, I am moved to deep gratitude and see the changes I must make.

There is grace abundant for all who fall short, pardon for those who come with hearts broken open to receive the good news of a world made new in Jesus Christ. Let, then, our hearts be broken. Let them be broken by the voices of God's people, crying out for the lives God has promised. Let them be broken by the witness of Jesus, who stood in the breach and cried aloud for those, his own people, wounded by the forces of domination and exploitation. Let them be broken by God's Spirit, who comes to disrupt, yes, but also to bind up, to create, to make order out of our chaos, beauty from our brokenness, so that the world may know the healing God desires. We will take down the corrupted structures on which we stand, and we will accept God's invitation to be partners in remaking the world.

*Straight*

# 2

# "Queer" Is Not a Four-Letter Word

I was as homophobic as any other straight, white, young adult male when I was in college. I used "gay" as a pejorative term for anything uncool or unwanted, I exchanged sideways glances when in the presence of someone I was sure was transgender, I made jokes about the latent homosexuality that must be present in the hazing rituals of the fraternities on campus which, according to rumor, seemed to almost involve touching one another's genitals. I understood "gay" as undesirable before I even really knew what the word meant.

I was a sheltered kid when I entered middle school, late to all of the worldly things my peers had already grasped. In fifth grade, I heard some classmates talking about Vanilla Ice's "Ice Ice Baby"—the biggest hit on the radio, but I had not heard it—and asked one of them who sang it. She sarcastically answered "Michael Jackson"—and I not only believed her but repeated it to a friend, who laughed in my face. If you wore the wrong thing, liked the wrong kind of music, sat or stood the wrong way, the accusations about being gay started, and I was guilty of all of the above. Almost all of these things had to do with being effeminate in any way; if you sat like a girl sits or stood like a girl stands, liked music that wasn't "masculine" enough, that label was headed your way. I barely knew what sex was, much less that it was possible to be attracted to someone with the same genitalia as you—which means that before I had any knowledge, I had prejudice.

As I got older, if you had caught me in a serious moment and presented me with the facts about the harm that anti-LGBTQ+ bias has done and is doing, explained to me what the letters in that acronym mean, and then asked me if I believed in equal rights and equal access for those who identify as LGBTQ+, I would likely have been moved to agree. Even in ignorance, I am generally inclined to err on the side of compassion; maybe you are too. But internalized anti-LGBTQ+ bias runs much deeper than that, which is why it is so important to seize opportunities to mine the sources of that bias and remove it from our consciousness as best we can. As is the case with patriarchy and white supremacy, there are the aspects of LGBTQ+ bias we can see clearly and name, and then there are the unconscious ways this bias shapes our thoughts and actions. To have healthy relationships with members of the LGBTQ+ community, to be trusted as allies and advocates, we will need to have done our own internal work, so that we can live with integrity.

I began to reevaluate my bias when I was in divinity school, as my friends and classmates were beginning their journeys toward ordination within their respective ecclesial bodies. There were a few whose gifts and abilities were inspiring, who gave me hope for the church at a time when each of us entering ministry was acutely aware that we were taking the mantle of leadership when profound shifts were happening within the institutional church. All of us knew that ministry would require more creativity and entrepreneurship than it had of the generation that had gone before, and that leading the church in this time of transformation would be no small task.

There were a few peers I looked up to—people who made me feel that we would all be all right. In the midst of our time in the program, one of those friends and classmates came out as gay. Those of us closest to them were not surprised, but we all knew what it meant—one of our friends, with the clearest gifts for ministry and greatest passion for their denomination, would likely not be ordained to Christian ministry. To me, this made no sense. It is not as if the church is swimming in leaders who both love the church and are equipped to serve at such a time as this. I thought of all the people this person would have loved well as a pastor; all the creativity and ingenuity they would have brought to leading the church; how much they loved the institution itself, which can be a qualification for seeking not just its survival but its flourishing. All of those possibilities tossed aside, excluded, because of one aspect of this person's identity.

It was then that this conversation came into greater clarity for me and, in hindsight, the moment when I began working to undo the anti-LGBTQ+ bias within me. I remembered my inherent bias when I was first approached to perform the wedding ceremony of a gay couple and wondered what my congregation would say. I remembered it when I sat on the ecclesial body that had the power to approve or deny candidates for ordination. I remembered it when my own children were born and I began to wonder about their gender identity or sexual orientation. There is so much I have taken in that must be purged, and the place to begin is confession—telling the truth about where I've been, where I am, and where I want to go.

My guess is that a good many of you have been formed in similar ways—in locker rooms and fraternity houses where masculinity and heterosexuality take on particular forms and must be proven, and in experiences that, intellectual reasoning and understanding aside, still create unease about other people's gender identity and sexuality. It is entirely likely that, if you have attended a Christian church, you have been taught specific ideas about what the Bible says with regard to gender and sexuality, and have seen these conversations take on outsized importance given their relative emphasis within the Bible itself. Those of us who have spent any time in the church have known this subject as a dividing line, a defining characteristic of a church's identity. Indeed, the primary voice opposing the growing rights of LGBTQ+ people in our culture is Christian, and these Christians come armed largely with a rigid (and, I would argue, inconsistent) view of Scripture. If we find the Bible authoritative for the way we understand God's desire for our life together, and if we believe that our interpretation of the Bible's message on these topics is problematic for loving and accepting LGBTQ+ people as they are, we will do the work to shed ourselves of our inherent biases.

I should say from the beginning that I am not a Bible scholar, and that when it comes to the few texts in Scripture that reference sexual activity between people with the same kind of genitals, I come to the text with a particular way of reading the Bible. First, I employ a helpful image that I picked up from Daniel Erlander's wonderful book *Manna and Mercy: A Brief History of God's Unfolding Promise to Mend the Entire Universe*.[1] Erlander explains that Jesus serves as a pair of eyeglasses through which we can see the whole of the biblical witness. That is, when viewed through the lens of Jesus, some things come into sharper focus and some things remain on the periphery—still present, but not the object of one's focus. This rings true for me as well, and it seems to me that if gender and sexuality were such a prominent and pressing issue for Jesus, he would have spent as much time teaching on the subject as he did the distribution of wealth, for example.

Second, the characterization I have of God is shaped by the whole of the biblical story and not necessarily a few texts. The pattern I see unfolding in the Bible is the abuse and misuse of power resulting in the exclusion and suffering of some, and God's intervention on behalf of those people so that the depth of God's love for all can be restored or established. In the Bible, those excluded, suffering people are often identified as widows and orphans, immigrants, the sick, hungry, imprisoned, rejected, or oppressed. When I consider who are the excluded and suffering in my own time and place, LGBTQ+ children of God who have had to fight so hard to insist on their humanity certainly qualify. It is difficult for me to imagine the God I have come to believe in sanctioning the acrimonious exclusion of people from the family of God based on their sexual orientation or gender identity, but having sufficient grace and forgiveness for those who continue to accumulate and compound wealth while so many suffer.

Third, I believe the context in which the text was written matters when interpreting Scripture, and to that end, it is difficult for me to conceive of first-century norms around sex applying to the significant cultural evolution that has taken place over the centuries. We do not keep concublnes, fur example. We believe in consent and have a prescribed age at which we believe consent can be given at all. We believe that love is part of meaningful sex. We have much more developed understandings about the physiology and chemical components of intercourse—how our bodies respond, the attachments they make, and the chemical interactions that shape our behavior. We accept this reality about all kinds of other biblical themes, including cleanliness, diseases, and mental illness, to name a few. We don't believe that a physical ailment represents some kind of spiritual deficiency and don't treat mental illness as demon possession. And yet, we are still clinging to Scripture as a way of proving that there is something irredeemably broken about our LGBTQ+ siblings, because a book written in a time and place with drastically different ideas about sex makes some somewhat ambiguous statements about it that we don't fully understand. There is more to our anti-LGTBQ+ bias than a rigid view of Scripture, but this is as good a place as any to begin.

## ANTI-LGBTQ+ BIAS IS A MISREADING OF SCRIPTURE

While preparing to write this chapter, I carried around a copy of Mark D. Jordan's book *The Invention of Sodomy in Christian Theology*. The cover is . . . not subtle. Every word in the title is in small print except "sodomy," which is printed in large capital letters across the front. This is an invitation for some interesting looks in the coffee shop.

The story of Sodom and Gomorrah in Genesis and how it has been understood over the years reveals something about our preoccupation with sexual contact between people of the same biological sex. In the story in Genesis 18–19, Abraham and his wife Sarah are visited by three divine "messengers." The couple's extravagant hospitality leads the visitors to extend to her the promise of a child, for which Abraham and Sarah have waited many years. The three messengers then set out toward Sodom, the city where Abraham's nephew Lot lives and which the Lord has told Abraham will be destroyed for its "grave sin." After the messengers of God arrive at Lot's house, the men of the city press in on the house and ask Lot to bring the men outside so that they might "know" them—that is, rape them. Lot offers his daughters, whom he touts as virgins, but the men of the city overpower him, at which point the messengers blind the Sodomite men so Lot and his family can escape.

This was enough to ensure the destruction of Sodom, and from this event we draw the word "sodomy," which has come to mean sexual intercourse other than vaginal penetration, and the word "sodomite" as a term for gay men. Mark D. Jordan, in his historical analysis, finds no reference to the term "sodomy" until the eleventh century, which, relative to the writing of Genesis, makes the term a relatively new invention.[2] It should be said—to my point above—that what is being threatened in this story is rape: violent, nonconsensual sex. Somehow, we have equated this act to the loving, consensual act of sex between two men.

Moreover, most of the references to the sin of Sodom in other parts of the Bible overwhelmingly name Sodom's sin as abuse of foreigners and other vulnerable people—a very specific kind of disobedience that the prophet Ezekiel clearly states: "This was the guilt of your sister Sodom: she and her daughters had pride, excess of food, and prosperous ease, but did not aid the poor and needy. They were haughty, and did abominable things before me; therefore I removed them when I saw it" (Ezek. 16:49–50). Perhaps, then, "sodomy" could be said to mean something entirely different from what we normally have understood, the definition that brought about those surprised looks in the coffee shop. Perhaps we should say that sodomy is rejection of the foreigner, the accumulation of wealth and privilege while others suffer. Occasionally I've heard folks say that the judgment of God will be on America for its embrace of the sin of sodomy. If we can agree that the sin of sodomy has more to do with the rejection and abuse of the foreigner, I am inclined to believe they're right.

There are, of course, other biblical texts that have been read to condemn sex between two people of the same gender: Leviticus 18:22 and 20:13; 1 Corinthians 6:9–10; 1 Timothy 1:10; and Romans 1:26–27. Scholars make compelling arguments on both sides of interpretation; again, I cannot interpret these passages to address loving, committed relationships between consenting adults, given the contexts in which they are found, which seem to address abusive or uncontrolled sexual activity rather than our modern sensibilities around sex as a meaningful, intimate loving act between two people.

If the Bible is (consciously or subconsciously) part of the reason for straight men's bias against LGBTQ+ people, perhaps this is because we have limited the scope of the passages within the Bible that we use to discern what faithfulness requires. All of us read the Bible with a hint of confirmation bias; that is, we hear it say what we hope it will say to confirm beliefs we already hold about God, ourselves, and others. If you go to the Bible looking for it to confirm a bias against a nonbinary understanding of gender, you may find it. If we open our minds to the whole of the biblical witness and consider what it has to tell us about justice for those who are marginalized and God's determination to offer the gift of belonging to those we have excluded, there are other biblical passages to which we may turn in thinking about the inclusion of our LGBTQ+ siblings.

I have frequently thought about Philip's interaction with the Ethiopian eunuch in Acts 8 as a justification for LGBTQ+ inclusion in Christian community. The eunuch was a member of the court of the Ethiopian queen Candace; eunuchs had their genitals removed to avoid the appearance of impropriety with the queen and were considered not entirely male or female. Without hesitation, Philip jumps into the eunuch's moving chariot, interprets Isaiah for him, and baptizes him then and there. I have often lifted up the eunuch's gender and sexual identity as evidence that God's communities are open even to those whose identities deviate from the norm, but I now believe this is a misreading, or at least a way of perpetuating norms rather than challenging them. It is not that God embraces the eunuch despite their flaws; instead, God does not regard this "flaw" at all, since the only obstacle to the eunuch's belief in Isaiah's prophecy is an understanding of who Jesus of Nazareth is and what he came to do and be. It seems to be no more important to the text that the new believer is a eunuch than it is that they are an Ethiopian or a member of the queen's court. Sometimes, even in working to undo our blind spots, we stumble upon more.

Our attempts at deeper understanding and acceptance can often go astray. Frequently I have heard Christians say things like "Well, I don't believe being gay is a choice," "No one would choose to be gay," or "They can't help who they're attracted to." I know Christians have said it, because I've participated in conversations like this myself, even parroted some of those lines. To say that being gay "can't be helped" or that experiencing gender fluidity is some kind of failure of biology implies that these identities are inherently defective. To say—as I have—that being gay is "not a choice" and that I cannot imagine a God who would condemn someone for something they did not choose is to say that LGBTQ+ folks are made broken—or made more broken somehow than the rest of us, who are also here trying to sort out how to be the most faithful versions of ourselves.

For me, a guiding passage on this subject of bias—toward LGBTQ+ individuals or anyone else—has been the interaction of Peter and Cornelius in Acts 10. Specifically, Peter is given a vision in which God commands him to cross a boundary the Law had created in order that Cornelius and his household,

Gentiles, may come to see and believe. Two things about this passage seem significant for this particular conversation: one is that God continues to speak, to move, to form the kindom of God even after Jesus has physically departed from the disciples. It is not Jesus who gives authoritative instruction in this matter—though certainly Jesus nudged us in this direction—but Peter hears directly from God. Admittedly, I have a lower theology of the apostolic tradition than others may, but I believe this passage serves as a reminder that God continues to speak in the interest of expanding the family of God, and can and will use ordinary human beings like Peter, like me, like you, to do it. Second, Peter is called on to change his mind about something he believes is settled. It is possible that God will send us to the very people we were once sure did not belong in the family of God. Who are we to say that the movement for LGBTQ+ inclusion in the church—including emerging generations who find this question repugnant and irrelevant—is not the Spirit of God inviting us to change our minds where once they were settled?

## ANTI-LGBTQ+ BIAS IS ABOUT PATRIARCHY

When you believe that the feminine is lesser and weaker than and subservient to the masculine, perhaps the worst thing a man can do is take on the role of a woman. If we believed that "feminine" qualities are of equal value, that the feminine is also strong, brave, assertive, and independent, why would it be so terrible to possess those qualities? Much of our LGBTQ+ bias is about defending patriarchal gender values; in the process a deep fear of emasculation is revealed. The patriarchy—the idea that man's rightful place is in leadership and woman's in supporting and being subservient to that leadership, which I will take up in much greater detail later—is constructed so that it can perpetuate itself. Young boys learn that there are certain qualities that go with being masculine, and vice versa for young girls. For boys in particular, a lot is riding on our ability to conform to those norms, including the self-esteem and assurance that comes with being the kind of man who is accepted by other men. In response, bullying toward any man who dares to buck patriarchal norms is especially severe, such that even the bullying itself is a means of proving one's masculinity. If I am particularly harsh toward the perceived effeminate man in the group, then I cannot possibly be effeminate myself.[3]

The particularly violent hatred of gay men or trans women by straight, cisgender men is rooted in this apparent betrayal of patriarchal values. To take on the role of a woman, when the underlying assumption is that women are less than, is seen as the strongest form of rejection. This kind of performative masculinity presents itself in all kinds of silly ways, including identifying particular causes—care of the environment or the rejection of militarism—as effeminate. Jared Yates Sexton tells the story of gathering at a family dinner, where the men in the room began to critique antiwar activism. When he spoke up to disagree with them, a string of epithets came forth, familiar names that show the close association between patriarchy and anti-LGBTQ+ bias: "pussy," "queer," and "f——" (redaction mine).[4] To refuse the stereotypes of masculinity, one must be either gay or a woman, and both are apparently bad.

Lesbians present a different kind of threat to the masculine sense of self. The idea that a woman may not find need of a man's protection, provision, or genitals is a threat to the ego that drives so much of the patriarchal mind-set. Patriarchy invites men to define themselves largely by their relationships to women—to assert our "leadership" over the women in our lives and win their deference as acknowledgment that our authority is needed. A woman who finds fulfillment in a relationship that does not include a man challenges this concept of power between genders, and even our sense of identity and self-worth, if this is the area of our lives we count on to make us feel worthy and capable.

One response to this perceived threat is to reduce these relationships to a fetish, a characterization that reduces relationships between two women to the act of sex itself, rather than a holistic way of discovering the gifts of love and grace in mutual relationships. If it cannot be fetishized, it is often derided as a kind of faux masculinity and given its own set of slurs and diminishing language.

If I am honest, I have harbored fear about the sexual orientations of my children, anxiety that they may be gay. I would like to say that this fear is related to the social consequences they would endure if they were, but I cannot say that with any confidence. To be clear, this is a fear that I am ashamed of. I know it is a vestige of anti-LGBTQ+ bias deep within me, but it is also a product of the patriarchal values I absorbed before I knew enough to resist them. At its root, I seem to believe that if my boys were gay, they would fail to be men, and that this would be some kind of indictment of me, their father, that I did not impress upon them an appropriate understanding of what it means to be a man. Intellectually, I understand that this could not be further from the truth, that if I act according to these fears I could do them harm. I am resolute that no matter whom my boys love, they will know that they have my love and acceptance, whatever toxic inward struggle I am dealing with.

Again, these are not ideas I am proud of, but I want to model the confessional approach I'm advocating in this book. I offer this because even those of us who are striving toward understanding and acceptance of that which is unfamiliar to us possess habits, ways of thinking, and irrational hopes and fears we will have to overcome, and it is likely that cannot be done by sheer force of will. It takes a community of care and support to find sobriety, a helpful metaphor Jared Yates Sexton offers.

Sexton writes, "Toxic masculinity is a chronic illness, and once we're infected we always carry it with us."[5] Later, he compares it to an addiction: "Like an addict who gets their addiction under control, I learned to view masculinity as a chronic problem I could never be totally cured of. Every day was a new struggle, as there was no such thing as conquering it. I knew, from previous experience, the easiest thing in the world would be to sink back into those destructive and dangerous behaviors."[6]

Overcoming addiction is a useful image. Patriarchal tendencies inform an anti-LGBTQ+ bias that even mindfulness cannot overcome. The first step is admitting we have a problem. Part of that problem is that we have internalized patriarchal values that see anything other than the masculine ideal as being of lesser value; and there really is no one we will not harm, including ourselves, to avoid risking having that patriarchal status taken from us.

## ANTI-LGBTQ+ BIAS GETS SEX
## AND GENDER WRONG

We tend to crave binaries: heroes or villains, Black or white, right or wrong, gay or straight, male or female. Binaries help us to make sense of the world we live in, to categorize things quickly and organize our way of seeing the world. The problem is that very few binaries really exist. You could try, for example, to categorize good guys and bad guys in the Bible, but you wouldn't get far. Which is King David, the adulterer, murderer, and hailed royal ancestor of Jesus? Which is Moses, fugitive from a murder charge and deliverer of God's people? Which is Paul, oppressor of God's people turned evangelist? Or Jesus himself, both fully human *and* fully divine? Binaries fall apart quickly. In the beginning, we believe that God created night and day, two binaries; but what of the time just before the sun peeks over the horizon, or the twilight just before it sinks below it? We believe there is land and sea, two binaries—but what of the space where the waves crash and are drawn back into the sea, where waves wash over rocks, where islands appear only when the tide falls? There are many in-between spaces, and often these are the places where we find the most beauty.

Likewise, we increasingly understand that gender and sexuality do not exist as fixed, binary absolutes, but as varied and fluid expressions of our humanity. For example, it was not until the nineteenth century that sexologists began classifying and categorizing sexual behaviors. Before this, the kind of sex you had, whom you were attracted to, the circumstances of the sex you had, and so on, all had moral implications as behaviors but were not understood to be determinative of a particular identity.[7] This is a relatively recent phenomenon, which we will take up in greater detail below. Naturally, when we began to classify sexuality, we began to make value judgments about what is normal and abnormal.

You may see similarities to the project of whiteness, or racial classification, which eventually led to the "one drop" rule. Anyone with "one drop" of African American ancestry was considered Black for the purposes of the racial hierarchy, in which whiteness was considered superior to all that was not white. Likewise, we began to make value judgments about sexual identities and practices—what constituted "good" sex and what was "bad," or abnormal, even if it took place within the traditional confines of marriage, which Christians have held is a necessity for sex to be a moral act.[8] However, who decides what is normal or abnormal? There are inherent dynamics of power at work here; I am inclined to believe that my expression of my sexuality or gender is entirely normal, and if I am in a position to make that standard determinative for others, I draw the boundaries with myself on the inside.

In a 2016 study, the Centers for Disease Control found that 17.4 percent of women ages 18 to 44 reported having same-sex sexual contact. Seven percent of men reported some form of sexual attraction to other men.[9] One might say that this constitutes a small minority, making same-sex attraction very much the exception rather than the rule, but it depends entirely on why and from what position you are making that judgment. For example, 10 percent of the population is left-handed, and most of us would be unsurprised to meet someone who is left-handed. It is worth asking why we are far more willing to ostracize and marginalize something fairly common, simply because it relates to sexuality.

In sum, the conclusions we reach about sex and gender, from which we make moral conclusions that mean inclusion or exclusion in our communities of faith, are not often grounded in human realities or honest about our own experience of being human. Who we are as sexual beings evolves over time, and the way we live into our particular gender identity is also fluid, depending on the social and cultural dynamics in which we find ourselves. This seems like shaky ground on which to decide on another's experience of God's love and care in Christian community.

## ANTI-LGBTQ+ BIAS IS DEHUMANIZING

Our fixation on sexual and gender norms has led us to give these particular aspects of our lives outsized importance in who we are as human beings. I'm attracted to women, but this is far from the most interesting thing about me (in my opinion). It does not take into account my guilty pleasure (true crime shows), my most fervent interests (sports, especially the Tar Heels), the type of music I enjoy, the food I like, the opinions I hold, the knowledge I have, the skills I possess; why, if my sexuality is not determinative for me, must that be the case for someone else? To reduce any of us to one aspect of our lives denies the fullness of our humanity.

The effect of this aggressive and skewed approach toward these children of God has been tragic. It must be said that the church has had a hand in the permanent estrangement of children from their parents because of moral claims I hope I have already shown to be flimsy, at best. On social media, you can see images of adults of a certain age offering "Mom" or "Dad" hugs to young people who have lost love and acceptance from their parents, the people we count on most to provide them. These scenes are both beautiful and tragic; beautiful, because neighbors are willing to offer this kind of restorative act, and tragic, because it has frequently been the church who created the need for it, and because these moments had to happen outside the church.

Among the general population in the United States, 4.6 percent of people have self-reported a suicide attempt.[10] LGBTQ+ youth seriously consider suicide at four times the rate of heterosexual youth.[11] A staggering 41 percent of adults who are transgender or gender nonconforming have tried to kill themselves.[12] Each time an LGBTQ+ person is harassed or abused because of their sexuality or gender identity, the likelihood increases by about 2.5 times on average.[13] The environment that the church has had such a prominent role in creating in this country has had deadly consequences.

These statistics come to mind each time I see a denominational body debating the question of same-sex "inclusion" as a matter of policy. Each time this occurs, there are people in the audience, young and old, who are listening as others debate, openly, their identity as beloved children of God. I wonder if these debates will engender thoughts of self-harm among them, and I am befuddled at the church's willingness to continue its outsized pursuit of this question, fully aware of the ruinous consequences. It is purely a miracle of God's grace and a testament to the movement of the Holy Spirit that any of our LGBTQ+ siblings even remain to hear the answers to the questions.

We take for granted where the church can be found. We tend to think that the church has a building, gatherings it calls worship, a staff, a website, a board, a constitution. We know that the communities that Jesus gathered to himself were frequently made up of those who had been rejected by the culture in which they lived, people whose identity had been identified as undesirable and become the catalyst for their marginalization. These are the people among whom Jesus lived, the reason for the spaces that Jesus created. That being the case, I wonder if the church is more easily found in the places we assume, or among the gathered community of those the church has disowned and disavowed, called unworthy, and asked to be less than who God made them to be. I think I go to church, but maybe the church of Jesus Christ is really unfolding at the pride parade.

## ANTI-LGBTQ+ BIAS IS HYPOCRITICAL

Earlier in this chapter, within the space of one or two lines, I listed the scriptural references we believe pertain to sexual acts between people of the same sex. I could do no such thing with the numerous scriptural references that warn against the accumulation of wealth, the oppression of the poor, the rejection of the foreigner, or the worship of false idols. And yet, the wealthy occupy our pews, Christians vote for politicians who create hostile environments for immigrants, and countless churches display American flags in close proximity to their altars. As Bishop William J. Barber frequently says, we have so much to say where the Bible says so little and so little to say where the Bible says so much.

We will ask questions about the bedrooms of those in our communities—actually, only the LGBTQ+ folks—but we are much more private about our bank accounts, our workplaces, and the rest of our home lives. In Acts, Luke tells us that the Christian community held all things in common, so that none had too much and none had too little. Accountability to this communal life was important; indeed, it held grave consequences for Ananias and Sapphira. In Acts 5:1–11, we hear how they sold a piece of property and withheld some of the proceeds from the community. In a confrontation, Peter accuses Ananias of lying not only to the others in the church, but also to God. At this Ananias falls down and dies. In short order his wife, Sapphira, approaches. She is not aware of what has happened and she too lies about the amount they received for the land. Peter calls for those who had carried off her husband and she promptly also dies.

Can you imagine, at your next stewardship campaign, having this passage read aloud and interpreted with the kind of literalism that is frequently applied to the passages in Leviticus or Romans to condemn sex between two people of the same gender? Can you imagine asking the members of your church to turn over their bank statements, for a thorough audit of their giving to the church? Or their credit card statements, for a full analysis of where they spend their money and on what? The pews would empty, and promptly, though this is far more biblical and has greater implications for the work of justice and equity Christ calls us to do, but it would never happen because it would affect too many of us. Those who find themselves in the majority—even when behaviors that are not in keeping with the teachings of Jesus are themselves the common thread that make them the majority—create justifications for themselves and use their power to oppress the minority. In Matthew 7:3, Jesus asks his audience, "Why do you see the speck in your neighbor's eye, but do not notice the log in your own eye?" There is always danger at hand when the majority are invited to decide on the basic human dignity of the minority.

In my own region of the Christian Church (Disciples of Christ), it was once suggested that the body charged with examining candidates for ordination should be required to ask about a candidate's sexual orientation before they were approved for ordination in the church (this, from the same denomination that ordained cult leader Jim Jones). Graciously, I was not asked this question. I was also not asked about my sexual past or present; I was not asked for my views on the use of violence, personal or corporate; I was not asked for my net worth (which would have been a negative number!), not even asked if I'd ever uttered a racial slur. Again, we isolate one (dis)qualification above all others, despite there being little biblical reason for believing it might be important to one's ability to serve the church.

If we will not see the inherent hypocrisy in our treatment of our LGBTQ+ siblings, others will. It is no coincidence that when one of our sister churches officially became open and affirming, they began to grow most noticeably among young families—not only LGBTQ+ families, but all families. For many younger people, questions about the inclusion of LGBTQ+ people are more or less settled. We have realized that people living out who they believe God has called them to be, as long as it is not harmful to their neighbors, is really not worth fighting about, especially given that we have so many,

many other patterns both inside and outside the church that continue to do harm to others, to ourselves, and to God's creation. There are certainly moments when the church is not called to go along with cultural mores, but we sure have chosen the wrong ones. When the people outside the church can see the planks in our eyes that we cannot see, it is time to take another look, open our minds, and open our hearts.

## ANTI-LGBTQ+ BIAS IS AN ABUSE OF POWER

To return to the example of the percentage of the population who are left-hand dominant, consider the various obstacles they face because ordinary tasks are oriented in favor of people whose right hand is dominant: using standard scissors, hunching in school desks attached on the right side, bumping elbows while eating at a table with mostly right-handed people, operating zippers and the numerical keypad on a keyboard with their nondominant hand. These are practical annoyances, created by a world oriented around the majority. The minority must either deal with these inconveniences or seek out solutions designed specifically for them.

The ways in which our culture has been oriented around cisgender, heterosexual people have far more serious and harmful implications. We are not so far removed from gay and lesbian couples being unable to legally marry and therefore unable to claim the tax benefits and health insurance coverage that often accompany that legal standing. Battles in local school districts are ongoing, as many fight to deny access and protections for LGBTQ+ students.[14] Only twenty-two states (and the District of Columbia) have laws prohibiting discrimination based on sexual orientation or gender identity, though they do not apply to churches.[15] Those of us in the majority have the power to declare whatever qualities we possess normative and force those who do not possess them to identify themselves in the negative—by what they do not possess and who they are not, instead of by who they are—and along the way we create ways of living, governing, and practicing our faith that privilege who we already are. Ultimately, how we use this power is a choice—we can choose to celebrate the various expressions of love and personhood we humans discover, or punish those who do not conform, in pursuit of a false sense of sameness. Too often, we continue to choose the latter.

When I heard human rights activist Ruby Sales speak at the Wild Goose Festival in the summer of 2018, she called the word "inclusive" into question. Inclusivity implies power. It assumes you have the power to include me or exclude me, but often when we use the word "inclusive" we are talking about spaces where we do not have rightful ownership.[16] Straight white men have a sense of ownership that has run amok.

There are boundaries within the church; there is a sense in which we must decide who and what is welcome in our practice of sacred Communion, who is qualified for leadership (both lay and ordained), what our values are as a community, but we are called to approach belonging in the family of God with a sense of humility. The apostrophe in the term "the Lord's Table" indicates the possessive—the Table belongs to Jesus Christ and not to us. When we draw lines to keep others out, God often takes up residence on the other side, moving among those we have cast out. We are invited to cross over and join God there.

# 3

## *So That All Means All*

At a 2015 conference sponsored by Bishop William J. Barber's organization, Repairers of the Breach, Bishop Tonia Rawls presented an interpretation of the story of Noah and the ark that I'd never heard before.[1] Bishop Rawls is a pastor and an activist in many areas, including LGBTQ+ rights. She asked us to imagine Noah standing at the door of the ark, and the challenges he must have faced, given the vocation to which God had called him. Can you imagine a lion coming up the gangplank to board? A giraffe? A rattlesnake? How would he care for them? How uncomfortable was he? Did he feel threatened, ill equipped, overwhelmed? At what point do you imagine he was tempted to close the door? Yet the door remained open and all manner of every living thing came into the place God had set aside for the preservation of life, for safe harbor in the midst of the storm that would rage outside.

Noah's job was simply to welcome those who came and to care for them, to offer them the same sanctuary he would share with his own family. He did not get to pick and choose who could come (cockroaches come to mind as one creature you might leave behind) but simply welcomed and cared for those

God sent. His job was to keep them alive, until the breach that formed between God and God's people had closed, and a covenant was made that would spare the world from this kind of judgment in the future. The covenant was sealed, of course, by a rainbow. Bishop Rawls encouraged us to begin to see LGBTQ+ folks with different eyes. We don't get to pick who comes; we just get to welcome the ones God sends, and keep them alive.

## BE CURIOUS, NOT JUDGMENTAL

This is technically a quote by Walt Whitman, but I am much fonder of Ted Lasso's interpretation (from the Apple TV+ show of the same name). In the show, Jason Sudeikis plays an American football coach hired by an English Premier League soccer team to be its head coach. The team's owner, recently divorced, is out to undermine the success of the team to spite her ex-husband, Rupert. In one of the best scenes, Lasso finds himself in the same sports bar with Rupert, who is mocking the team's struggles and promises to attend every game to mock Rebecca, his former wife.[2] Ted makes a wager over a game of darts; if he wins, Rupert stays away. As he takes his turn, Ted needs a nearly impossible combination to win. As he begins, he quotes Whitman—"be curious, not judgmental"—and talks about all the people who have doubted him over the years, all the people who judged him without stopping to know him, to ask questions, to be curious about who he is. For example, he says, you might have asked if I've ever thrown any darts, and I could have told you yes, that I'd thrown them all the time in the sports bar with my dad. Then he promptly throws the winning bull's-eye. It's the most inspirational kind of hustle.

Coach Lasso's point is that we often form judgments without knowledge. Christians have perhaps made more judgments with less knowledge about LGBTQ+ people than they have about anything else. Now, we understand that some of these are ridiculous (at least I hope we do): the ideas that sexual orientation is somehow linked to pedophilia, that sexual orientation can be changed with the right kind of therapy, that LGBTQ+ folks have some kind of "agenda" that involves a slow takeover of the culture at large. Language and understanding around gender and sexuality are constantly evolving, which means that there is likely something we accept as true at this moment that will soon enough be understood differently and more fully.

People of faith still study a Bible that has not substantially changed in centuries, and we still look for new insights, interpretations, and knowledge that will give us a deeper and more fully formed faith. It stands to reason that we might also commit ourselves to knowing and understanding our neighbors—the issues they face, the lives they lead, the joys they find. It is difficult to know how to love and care for someone if you do not know them.

It is possible, even likely, that you will learn something that makes you uncomfortable. The question is whether or not you believe the gospel values of welcome and hospitality make it worth enduring discomfort on your way to understanding. What do you know about being transgender? Perhaps there are trans people who would be willing to share with you, but as we will see when it comes to the experience of persons of color, the unique and often trying experience of marginalized people does not exist for your enlightenment. There are many, many ways to learn about those who experience this life differently without requiring them to endure our curiosity when it can be harmful. Read, listen, learn, stand corrected, and then learn some more.

## BE SPECIFIC

We must be clear about where we stand when it comes to welcoming and affirming our LGBTQ+ siblings. Many churches use ambiguous language about being "open to all" or "inclusive of everyone" when this is not the lived reality of that community. These churches are welcoming, but not affirming. That is, they are happy to have LGBTQ+ people worship with them, but they will not perform their weddings or invite them into leadership; they do not affirm them as they are. "All" doesn't really mean "all," in other words. Unfortunately, too many LGBTQ+ individuals and couples find this out only after they have become part of the community, built relationships, and grown familiar with the pastor and worship style. While it is true that many Christians choose churches because of the relationships they form and not the theology they hear preached and see practiced, those who believe that the church's practices around LGBTQ+ justice are important cannot afford to settle in a Christian community without making it a priority.

In the same way, if you are in a congregation that is ambiguous in its welcome of our LGBTQ+ siblings, urge the church to make its position clear. I have debated the importance of the title "open and affirming" in my own mind and with others. Some argue that taking on this title is unnecessarily divisive; if churches define themselves in this way, they exclude some (those who are not prepared to be personally open and affirming of those who identify as LGBTQ+) at the expense of others. My experience is that the language is important, and it is necessary to be specific. Too many LGBTQ+ churchgoers have made assumptions based on ambiguous language only to find that, in reality, that church is not a safe place for them. If we intend to welcome our LGBTQ+ siblings, we must say so, specifically, so that everyone knows what kind of community we intend to be. It is possible that some may leave when we take this step; but we are not on a search for the lowest common denominator of Christian belief, but for a fuller, deeper understanding of the gospel and what it demands of us in the time and place in which we live.

My denomination, the Christian Church (Disciples of Christ), has always prized unity, even calling unity our "polar star." In practice, this has too frequently meant an unhealthy aversion to conflict. Because we want to maintain our unity in Christ, we have resisted making more definitive theological statements, even when presented with an opportunity to place ourselves squarely in the fight for justice in our world. At our 2013 General Assembly in Orlando, Florida, voting delegates voted on a "sense of the assembly" resolution that expressly included our LGBTQ+ siblings among those welcome at the Lord's Table. To be clear, in our church polity, "sense of the assembly" resolutions have no binding effect on local congregations. They are exactly what they sound like—the consensus of those voting delegates gathered on that particular day, received as guidance for the rest of the church. The result, however, was much the same as if this had been binding. In my region, North Carolina, congregations seized on this reason to sever covenant ties to the denomination. Simply associating with other Christians who would make that kind of public proclamation of welcome was more than they could stomach.

As a denomination, we had discerned together, took a few steps toward entering the conversation on the side of LGBTQ+ justice, and still left room for others to be church in the way they felt was faithful, but it wasn't enough. In the end, those churches that held an anti-LGBTQ+ theology left anyway. We may as well have moved even more strongly in the direction of justice. Even if this step brings a season of conflict, if it is a clarifying moment for the community and for individuals who decide that this is no longer the best community for them, everyone has grown.

The congregation I serve has used language implying openness to the LGBTQ+ community but has not gone so far as to use explicit, expansive language in its statement of belief (as of this writing). This is not because there is not a desire among the people to welcome everyone; it is largely because of my desire for us to understand what we are saying when we say we are open and affirming of our LGBTQ+ siblings. Desiring to be open and affirming is a different thing from having taken the steps necessary to live into the label. It requires sufficient and ongoing curiosity about what this welcome means: how we avoid doing harm, what power structures we have in place that need to be rebuilt, what physical changes might be required in our space, what language we should change in the documents that organize the church structure. These are all questions a church that wishes to be open and affirming both in title and in practice must ask.

In the same way, language is not a once and for all solution. Every institution, after a period of expanding boundaries, can become entrenched behind them. Since our understanding of gender and sexuality are evolving, we can never abandon the work of discernment when it comes to who is welcome and how we share power. In the end, not every Christian community will be perfectly suited to every person, but living into the imperatives of the gospel and the example of the early church invite us to always be asking ourselves who is not here, and why. When we ask ourselves that clarifying question, we are more likely to see the ways that the norms we create and sustain exclude and confine. The more space we create for those around us to become the fullest expression of who they are, the more we become faithful partners with God in God's desire to see all God's children be free.

## ENOUGH WITH THE GENDER REVEALS

The latest arms race among expectant parents is the gender reveal celebration, wherein the mom- and dad-to-be invite their friends and family to some sort of ritualized way of announcing the sex of the baby, yet to be born. I use the term "arms race" because these are becoming more and more elaborate; google "gender reveal ideas" and you will find everything from simple to ridiculous and beyond. You can hit exploding golf balls filled with pink or blue powder, cut cakes with pink or blue filling, pop balloons filled with confetti . . . or, like one California couple, start a 10,000-acre wildfire with the pyrotechnic device used to reveal the genitalia spotted during the ultrasound.[3] Despite the elaborate attempts to be different, these mostly turn out the same: if the smoke (or confetti or icing or whatever) is pink, we all know "it's a girl," and if it's blue, "it's a boy."

What they reveal, in fact—since gender has less to do with anatomy and more to do with how a person perceives their identity at a personal and subconscious level—is the preconceived notions the expectant parents have about their children. Pink not only indicates female anatomy, according to our current cultural symbolism, but assumptions that the baby will grow into someone who wears dresses and hair bows, plays with dolls, and dates boys. Blue suggests not just a penis but a person who will play sports, like cars, and pursue women. Ultimately, these parties make particular statements about who we believe our children will be when they enter this world, become children with active imagination and curiosities, and grow into young adults. In this way, they're a setup for fractured relationships between parents and children because—as any parent should be able to tell you—we rarely get the children we expect. This can be a wonderful, evolving, continual blessing, or a place of pain and consternation in one of the most sacred relationships this life offers us.

It is possible you will have a boy who loves to play with dolls. It is also possible you will have a girl who prefers shorts and a T-shirt to a pink, frilly princess costume. What are we setting ourselves up for by deciding who our children will be before they have drawn their first breath? We parents do this enough; we envision what our children will look like, what they will act like, what they will be interested in, how their lives will turn out. This is natural, part of the excitement that comes with bringing new life into the world, knowing that this new life bears our DNA—something of the imprint of who we are—and that how we love and raise this child will shape who they become in profound ways.

In premarital counseling sessions, I often talk with couples about the values each one brings to the idea of parenting. In one of those sessions, a groom remarked that the great thing about children is that you can shape and mold them into how you want them to be. I could not contain my laughter. This is not how it works. Who is in charge, really? The one who is crying at two a.m., or the one who cannot sleep? The one who is beginning to smile, or the ones who are making fools of themselves to help the baby along?

As a parent, I learned early on that as much as I was shaping the behavior of my children, they were also challenging the way I saw the world and myself. And I learned that our children were formed in profound ways before I ever laid hands on them. One would not sleep unless one of us was lying next to the crib; the other would reach for the crib while we rocked, ready to be put down and left alone. We did not do this. It just was. And in those small ways, we learn that while we are shaping who our children will be, we are also learning to know them—and love them—as they are.

You can have set ideas about who your children should be; since you love playing sports, they should also love that, or since you love playing the piano, they will too. And perhaps, for a while, they will play along, because they know this makes you happy and wins your approval, and many children crave both of those things. Possibly you will help them discover their life's passion, or possibly they will one day resent the very thing you hoped they would love, because they somehow came to believe that you could only love the version of themselves that they were when they were in the batter's box or in the dance studio. None of us wants to be loved only on the condition that we can be someone we are not. We want to be loved because of who we are, and loved in a way that encourages us to be the most faithful version of that person we can be.

Those who are uncomfortable with the idea that sex (one's genitals) and gender (one's internal identity) may not align seem to believe that parents who are open to their child's self-determination in this area are doing harm. There are two genders, they argue, and this wasn't an issue until we gave children the idea that there's some kind of choice they have to make, which only serves to confuse them (and erode the order God established at creation). There are several problems with this way of thinking. First, gender diversity is not new. What is new is our ability to see and understand, the growing comfort our culture has with allowing people to be fully who they believe God made them to be, our ability to have this conversation in the open, instead of underground. Without this level of acceptance—still far from where it might be—instead we have led beloved children of God to self-harm, estrangement from those whose love they most covet, and other unhealthy ways of coping with what it means to live in a world where one does not belong. Second, every child goes through a state of confusion about who they are (often we call this puberty), and leading them to absolutes does not often mean clarity.

This discomfort betrays our general aversion to what cannot be categorized. Unfortunately, rather than equipping us for living with the gray areas of our lives, our faith has often been offered to us only in black-and-white terms. God is often assigned a gender, I believe, because we cannot conceive of that which cannot be categorized (and if we are going to categorize something to be worshiped, it should definitely be classified as a man).

How do we begin to think about God in terms that cannot be confined by the limits of bodies? Some of our ancestors in faith had an easier time with this than we do. Rabbi Mark Sameth, in a *New York Times* op-ed, points out that the Hebrew Bible is flexible in its use of pronouns: "In Genesis 3:12, Eve is referred to as 'he.' In Genesis 9:21, after the flood, Noah repairs to 'her' tent. Genesis 24:16 refers to Rebecca as a 'young man.' And Genesis 1:27 refers to Adam as 'them.'"[4] Sameth even says that the Tetragrammaton—the four-letter name for God in Hebrew, YHWH—might have been pronounced like the Hebrew words for "He/She." Those who wrote down our sacred text, whose conceptions of God and the action of God in human life form our own, were less bound by categories than we are.

We fire off blue or pink smoke or confetti in anticipation of births, but I wonder what would happen if, just once, it was purple. It would make for confusion, far less cheering, and no funny reactions that might help the festivities go viral. But it might speak more truth about the true excitement that comes with a life entering the world. This is not often an either-or life. More frequently, it is a both-and life. We will know more about this life, about God, about ourselves, if we make room for the in-between—from the very beginning.

## REPRESENTATION MATTERS

I am old enough to remember when Jerry Falwell claimed that one of the Teletubbies was gay.[5] The Teletubbies were giant costumed characters—who were not all that similar to humans—on a children's television show. They danced and sang and the whole production was of the sort that feels like a fever dream to adults but is somehow entertaining to small children. While Falwell's claim was (deservedly) laughed at and dismissed by many, it played on a common fear among the parents of Generation X and millennials that the media their children consumed somehow influenced their sexual orientation, as if a person in a weird costume could be determinative in this area. There were cultural voices, like Falwell, who did what they could to stoke this fear and encouraged parents to question the things their children consumed, in case they would acquire ideas their parents preferred they avoid. To a certain degree, it is right to think critically about what we consume—not because watching Teletubbies would make a child gay or lesbian, or that it would be terrible if it did, but because the images we consume shape our imaginations and can reinforce problematic norms and power structures within our wider culture. For this reason, children's programming is much different than it was when I was a child—there are cartoon characters of color who serve as positive role models for young children, young women who do not wait around for a man to come and save them, and so on—but the battle for this kind of representation has been contentious, and it has changed dramatically over time.

In one generation, we have witnessed a shift on television, from the backlash to Ellen DeGeneres coming out on her television sitcom *Ellen* in 1997, which resulted in its declining ratings and ultimate cancellation; to wildly popular shows like *Will and Grace*, which featured several gay characters; to the show *Schitt's Creek*, which explored more diverse expressions of gender and sexuality, without boycotts making mainstream news.

Representation in popular culture has helped our sensibilities around LGBTQ+ issues evolve. However, as noted in chapter 2, this has not translated to areas of our culture where power is held, especially the corporate world and local, state, and national political systems, not to mention the church. When LGBTQ+ people struggle to get promotions, are paid less than their cisgender, heterosexual peers, and are underrepresented in elected office, the voices of our LGBTQ+ neighbors are not often heard in places where power is held in our communities.

A 2020 study showed a significant increase in LGBTQ+ politicians running for public office, and winning; specifically, a 21 percent increase in elected officials from 2019 to 2020 alone.[6] However, it is easy to make exponential gains when the starting number is exceedingly low: only 0.17 percent of elected officials identify as LGBTQ+, while the figure for US adults is 4.5 percent.[7] Similarly, 0.3 percent of Fortune 500 CEOs openly identify as LGBTQ+,[8] despite at least anecdotal evidence that businesses with LGBTQ+ persons in senior leadership perform better overall.[9]

It is encouraging to see increased diversity and representation in music, television, and movies, and to see more companies acknowledging and participating in Pride Month, but these ultimately do not materially change the lives of LGBTQ+ people if they remain excluded from the rooms where policies are made and resources allocated. Herein lies the choice for straight, cisgender white men who are in political office, leading companies, making hiring decisions, and enforcing antidiscrimination policies. Perhaps the first step is learning to check our anti-LGBTQ+ bias—why it manifests itself, and how. A further step may be going about the work we do in ways that value the LGBTQ+ siblings among us, listening and advocating for their interests and needs.

There is a still greater step, one common to all of the identities taken up in this book, and that is ceding leadership (and therefore power) where we can to LGBTQ+ persons—not expressly because being LGBTQ+ is itself a qualification, but because it is difficult to create environments where everyone can flourish when not everyone who is part of the community is represented among those who shape how we live. Relinquishing the privilege that comes with not having to articulate your gender identity or worrying about whether your partner will be accepted by your family or friends means giving our seat at the tables where decisions are made to those most affected, most marginalized by our history of stigma and shame—because who leads matters, who's at the front matters, who's in charge matters, especially where meaningful change is needed. When we awaken to the worlds we have created and discover a desire to create new ones, new ways of living and sharing are what we need—new ways of seeing, thinking, and speaking.

## WATCH YOUR MOUTH

I resisted using the word "homophobia" in the previous chapter for a few reasons. First, because it excludes the prejudice and systematic oppression experienced by many in the LGBTQ+ community who do not identify as gay or lesbian. Second, because there is no such thing as "homophobia" in the sense of a diagnosable anxiety disorder like agoraphobia (fear of public places) or claustrophobia (panic induced by being cramped or confined spaces). I was once a young man who frequented locker rooms and dorm rooms. I know all about what we have frequently labeled as homophobia, and it isn't rooted in any kind of physiological response or genuine anxiety or fear. More accurately, it is just overt and vitriolic prejudice or bias, and language is both a cause and a symptom.

During my ministry, I have regularly worked in our camping ministry, where youth gather at our regional facility for a week of fun, fellowship, and hopefully some Christian formation. I vividly remember one conversation with a group of young people, after they'd heard a talk that urged them to reconsider how they use language that's unfortunately too common; "That's so gay!" as a pejorative statement, for example. This is a simple concept that required a surprising amount of discussion and redirection to get across. Finally, when I asked one of the young women, who had bright red hair, to reflect on what it might feel like to have "red hair" used in the same way, the concept seemed to click. Perhaps it's not good to make an aspect of a person's humanity also a term of derision.

We internalize what we hear and what we say, and our language has a profound effect on what (and who) we value. Because I learned—often from what was said to me and about me—that it was undesirable for a young man to have any of the traditionally understood characteristics of a woman, that it would cost me social currency to be thought of as gay, I internalized a certain feeling about sexual expressions and gender identities that felt foreign to me. We can often be afraid of what we don't understand, yes, but mostly the language that gives life to "homophobia" is about placing one's self on the "right" side of the social equation. The result of this socialization manifests itself in language, in attitude, and then almost certainly in action.

Two contrasting depictions from pop culture come to mind. The first is from *Friends*, the formative TV show of my generation. One of the running jokes that showed up again and again over the course of the show was that the character Chandler was often perceived as being gay, and the urgency with which he wished to set the record straight about his sexual orientation. In one episode, Ross and Joey fall asleep on the couch, only to wake up and find that they have been snuggled up to one another and enjoyed the best sleep of their lives.[10] At once they are afraid of the implications of two men touching each other, even in a way that has no sexual implications. Later, when they re-create the scenario intentionally (to try to have another epic nap), they are embarrassed when the rest of the friends discover them. The joke—presumably—was these straight men displaying mannerisms or engaging in behavior that apparently called their sexuality into question, their defensive reaction to being understood that way, and how undesirable that would be.

Contrast these depictions to the character of Michael Scott (played by Steve Carell) in *The Office*. His cluelessness about what is appropriate in an office environment is a defining trait of the character and a source of comedy. In some sense, his character is satirical, a commentary on the social issues facing American culture when the show was made, which still have currency some years later. In one episode (*Gay Witch Hunt*), Michael uses the word "faggy" in an attempt to mock Oscar, a coworker he believes is straight.[11] In fact, Oscar is a gay man who has chosen not to disclose his sexuality to his coworkers. When he is informed of Oscar's sexuality and questioned by the human resources rep about his language, Michael says, "I would've never called him that if I knew." The rest of the episode is a textbook example of cringe comedy, as Michael attempts to prove that he is comfortable with Oscar's sexuality after all, and that he wants to understand what he doesn't understand, even though his attempts to show it are misguided. The joke is not that Oscar is gay, or even that Michael is clueless about how offensive his words are; it is that Michael seems to desire a welcoming environment but is completely oblivious to his very apparent LGBTQ+ bias. In this way, he is an extreme example of how our language and our prejudice make actual workplaces hostile environments for LGBTQ+ folks, and holding up this caricature highlights how ridiculous the language and attitudes that characterize anti-LGBTQ+ bias really are. The nuance is important; the examples from *Friends* perpetuate harmful attitudes among that generation, and the example from *The Office* lifts up these attitudes in cartoonish ways that help us to see how problematic—and harmful—they are.

These depictions matter, in that they establish cultural sensibilities that inform the way we treat other people *and* reflect something of how we see one another. The *Friends* scenario mirrors language that smacks of patriarchy (in the sense that it is undesirable for men to be viewed as feminine) and anti-LGBTQ+ bias. It is true to life, but makes no artistic comment that invites us to imagine our relationships differently, which means it risks reinforcing them instead. What we say matters. Our words matter. In Genesis, God gives the first humans the task of naming the things they see around them, demonstrating what a sacred task it is to describe the world we live in—not to be taken lightly or done flippantly.

Unlearning patterns of speech (as that group of youth at church camp did) is one thing, but learning the vocabulary that goes along with honoring the presence of our LGBTQ+ siblings among us is equally essential. For example, sharing our pronouns in gatherings large or small spares those whose gender identity may differ from prescribed norms the isolation of being the only person to have to clarify their gender; in other words, we avoid highlighting what does not fit those norms, and work instead to deconstruct our ideas about stereotyped gender expression.

New language and best practices continue to emerge around different experiences of sex and gender, and if we want to welcome all of God's children into the fold of the loving community God has created, we must know how to speak to one another in ways that honor our mutual humanity. If this feels like hard work, perhaps you might consider how much time and energy you put into continuing your education in your chosen field—new technologies, strategies, and so on—then consider how important practicing the love of God for all people is by comparison.

## SEE THE WHOLE PERSON

Few of us want to be reduced to a stereotype. I wear my hair (the portion that still grows) closely shaved, with a beard that is frequently longer (and definitely thicker) than the hair on top of my head. Certain associations come with my appearance. You might assume I'm a fan of *Fast and Furious* movies (never seen one) or that I'm into smoking meat (that's true). Few of us can be reduced to the flat, uncomplicated versions of ourselves that stereotypes suggest, and we react viscerally to the suggestion that we can, because it denies fundamental aspects of who we are and how we see ourselves. But when we look at other people, something about us wants to take what is complex and diverse and sort it into neatly defined categories and demographics, about which we can make certain assumptions. We want to label and sort human beings as we do our spice cabinets, so that we can glance and decide what's on the inside without much work.

But we simply aren't those kinds of creatures. Given enough time, we surprise and confound one another, which is one of the gifts of being human—the journey toward understanding that we are all on, simultaneously working to know ourselves and, in the process, know those around us in ways that give our lives joy and meaning. We are not one thing or another all the time, and while certain roles we play in this life may take on defining importance, they rarely tell the whole story, and we do not live into these vocations in the way others might. For example, I would like to think I am a good father, but I often find myself comparing the way I relate to my kids to others around me who possess qualities I do not see in myself, which leads me to doubt the quality of my parenting. I tell myself that we are all dads, and we can all carry that mantle well without going about it the same way. This extends further—there is more than one way to be a man, more than one way to be a husband; many, many ways to express one's faith.

When see each person—really see them, in all their complexity and category-defying glory—we begin to see one another as God sees us. I've been afforded the luxury, in this culture, of not having my sexual orientation or gender identity become a primary marker by which others define me, make assumptions about me, decide that I should be ostracized, demeaned, or harmed. I do not think twice about how I express these aspects of who I am, and I assume others see me as much more than those things.

We owe each other the space to be the people we believe God made us to be, to find the fullest way we can to be our best selves, able to love and be loved, to give the best of who we are to those around us. Given that space, we discover dignity and self-worth and the gifts each of us possess for enriching the lives of those around us. When we deny others that space, ultimately we also deny ourselves—instead of siblings in Christ, we become oppressed and oppressor, powerful and dispossessed, when none of us is only our sexuality or our gender or our insecurity or our prejudice. To create that kind of space, we must resist the temptation to categorize one another by one single, defining characteristic—we must see the whole person. This, too, seems like hard work. We categorize for easy reference, so we can decide who someone is without wading into the depths of discovering all the contradictions that they possess. There is more to the person you notice in the midst of transitioning, more to the couple holding hands on the street; what a loss it would be to see only two dimensions in a three-dimensional world, full of all kinds of God's children, all of whom tell us something about the God we seek, in whose image we are made.

# Gay, White, and Male

## Trust Takes Time

MATTHIAS ROBERTS

If we ever see each other in person, I'll likely avoid you.

If we do interact, I'll smile, laugh, be pleasant, all the while attempting to regulate my heartbeat and not let my suspicion of you show through. I'll breathe easier once you are walking away. I don't trust you.

Mistrust in any sort of faith-based context (unless it is an exclusively queer space) seems like the standard in my life. There are few exceptions; it's built into my body. The mistrust is a warning alarm: *Be careful,* it says, *you don't know when you'll be blindsided.*

I could attempt to explain why I believe the response of mistrust is involuntary, why it takes effort for me to walk into ministry settings, even progressive ones, despite likely sharing similar beliefs. But these kinds of stories explaining why are unfortunately very easy to find. The trauma LGBTQ+ people face, especially in well-meaning church environments, is immense. I imagine you've heard some of these stories. If you haven't, how do you think you'll be able to take a healing posture without knowing the shape of our harm?

I hope chapters 2 and 3 have helped you explore the LGBTQ+ bias you may hold—consciously or subconsciously—and reconsider some of the biblical arguments and church positions that may have perpetuated that bias. I hope you are willing to adopt a posture of curiosity rather than judgment, because an important place where theory becomes action is in this realm of trust. Many LGBTQ+ people don't trust you, and building their trust will take work.

Social researcher and storyteller Dr. Brené Brown uses the metaphor of a marble jar to describe the process of building trust. In her book *Daring Greatly,* she suggests that building trust happens in small, everyday interactions.[1] Actions like remembering someone's birthday or texting a friend after an interview they were nervous about put marbles in the jar. Rarely is trust built through giant, grand gestures or statements; instead it's built by following through, by being dependable and considerate.

As white men, many of us are used to meeting people and automatically having that jar be somewhat, if not mostly, filled. By virtue of our social positioning, we are more often trusted than not. We get away with things. We become used to that. In some realm of our being, we believe we are trustworthy by default because that's how many people treat us. Thus, when we meet someone who doesn't trust us automatically, someone who is a bit suspicious of us, we take it as a personal offense. It can feel like a gut punch; it's an ego hit. That alone can keep us from entering into deep relationships with people in communities who don't extend to us the trust we are used to.

It's important to understand, if you are a straight white male, most LGBTQ+ people you meet will be approaching you with an empty jar. Queer people expect that if there's going to be a relationship, you'll do the work to put marbles in the trust jar. We're not going to automatically assume you've done that work, even if you tell us you have. You'll have to show us.

The process of earning trust is a difficult one, and in some ways it's tumultuous. It doesn't take much to knock the jar over and spill all the marbles, especially in the early days when the marble jar can feel like it's teetering on the edge of a windy cliff. This is one of the effects of working with a traumatized community: trust is harder to build. I often see people like you get tripped up here.

Here's an example: One day, I open my in-box and find an email from a pastor who is excited about doing LGBTQ+ justice work in the church. Let's name him Trent. Trent isn't a real person; he's an amalgamation of some of my experiences. He's a straight white pastor and has done his own research. He's read the right books, been to the right conferences, and is starting to meet a community of people who are as passionate as he is. He's serious about the work and asks me for advice: "How can I love the LGBTQ+ community better?"

Trent and I begin to build a relationship, and over the course of a year the reality of what it actually means to earn the trust of a community starts to settle in for Trent. He's done good work, he's begun to build friendships with LGBTQ+ people in his church, and he's taken actions to make his church a safer space for queer people. However, his initial excitement is wearing off and the generosity he was able to extend toward people who don't trust him starts to falter. Trent begins to be more visibly affected by the fact that people aren't extending him trust automatically in the ways he is used to.

He comes to me one day and says: "It feels like I'm pushing a boulder up a hill when all I want to do is love people!" At this point, Trent is getting more defensive, less willing to accept feedback from me, and far more likely to interject in our conversations long explanations about how he is doing the right thing. He'll start telling me stories about the ways he was harmed by gender norms growing up and how that uniquely qualifies him to understand queer people, if they'd only give him the chance. He's frustrated.

Eventually, Trent cracks, and one day he decides to be vulnerable during a meeting of queer congregants. All of the frustrations he's had, all the ego hits he's internalized from not feeling trusted, come spilling out in the form of "look at how hard I've worked." The queer people in the meeting shift uncomfortably. One or two of them attempt to empathize with Trent to help him feel less exposed, but underneath suspicions are being confirmed: This pastor is only in this work because it makes him feel like a healer, because it makes him feel helpful and important. The queer people hear Trent's message loud and clear: "You are hurting *me* because you don't know what it's like for me to do this work."

Now, in this example, it isn't true that Trent is only in this work for the ego gratification. While there's certainly an element of ego present, it's nearly impossible for there not to be when we feel as though we're called to a marginalized community. Trent is doing this work because he deeply believes it's part of God's work on this earth. He's in it because he knows LGBTQ+ equality is an element of doing justice and loving mercy. However, the damage has been done. The marbles that he had worked so hard to put in the jar have been spilled, and likely, the jar has been shattered.

All of this could have been avoided by Trent doing some of his own work on what it means to not be trusted. Trent could have worked with a therapist, or a trusted mentor, to unpack the ego hits that inevitably come. He could have vented along the way to a peer who is further along in this work, someone who could validate his frustration and continue to push him forward.

Here's a key point: Earning trust has as much to do with the posture you take toward yourself as it does with outward-facing action. If you're going to do this work, there will be times where you'll be furious and times when you feel unappreciated. There are going to be times where you need to express all your frustrations over how seemingly ungrateful, or picky with language, or untrusting LGBTQ+ folks are. That's to be expected.

But where I see this ruin people like you is when these things are left unprocessed, or when you feel that *we* are the people to process these things with. When you feel that you need to tell us, in direct or indirect ways, how grateful we should be for the work you are doing in this world, you are in dangerous waters. There are few things that will ruin all your hard-earned trust faster than taking this posture.

Thus, having people other than just LGBTQ+ people guide you in this work is vital. You cannot rely upon us exclusively, otherwise you'll likely fall into this trap. It happens time and time again, especially among white dudes. White men are the most susceptible to this, and I notice it within myself often while doing justice work, and even more often when working alongside pastors who meet these descriptions.

This is just one example of where I see folks getting tripped up in this work, but it is a significant one: trust has to be earned, especially when approaching LGBTQ+ people in faith communities. That fact in itself can trigger all kinds of internalized defensiveness because of the way white men have been socialized. White men are used to automatically being trusted, so undoing those assumptions and working with the defenses that get triggered is part of doing justice, too. When you've done that work, you'll likely notice LGBTQ+ people will become far less suspicious of you. And we'll maybe even stop avoiding you.

*White*

# 4

# *White Supremacy and the Air We Breathe*

My father had been a junior high history teacher before becoming a school administrator, and he encouraged a love of history in me, especially Civil War history. When the film *Gettysburg* came to theaters, I went to see it with him. At age thirteen, I sat through a 4-hour-and-31-minute film, complete with an intermission, about one Civil War battle. I remember watching that movie and—as a born-and-bred Southerner—finding myself rooting for the side in gray. I knew how it ended, and yet found myself frustrated with J. E. B. Stuart's unreliable scouting, and irritated by how much I liked Joshua Chamberlain (played beautifully by Jeff Daniels), who inspired his troops to hold the Union line against a relentless charge by the Confederates; I shook my head when Pickett led his troops out into the open field, knowing that it would be a turning point in the war. I didn't make the connection to what they were fighting for—only that my "team" was losing.

While minoring in history at University of North Carolina, I took a Civil War history course. On the first day of class, the professor took an informal poll. He asked who in the class believed the Civil War had been about something other

than slavery. Learning alternative reasons many of our ancestors went off to fight against their own government is a rite
of passage in the South. We learn phrases like "states' rights"
and "protecting the Southern way of life" and "the War of
Northern Aggression." Based on the hands that went up, there
was a fairly even divide between those whose study of history
to that point had grounded them in reality, and others who
were not ready to admit what all those phrases they'd learned
really meant.

We were only a few hundred yards from Silent Sam, the
university's monument to its Confederate dead, erected in
the early 1900s in a ceremony littered with violent white
supremacist language. We were even closer to the university's
first buildings, erected with slave labor. Over the course of the
semester, our professor undertook a systematic academic proof
of America's amplification of white supremacy to justify the
economic practice of stolen labor and intellectual property. We
learned about the brutality of the slave trade, the utter depen-
dence on slavery as a means to wealth and prosperity for white
landowners in the South, and how European economies and
the northern states also benefited. The professor brought us
face-to-face with the South's fight to preserve this unjust system of economic exploitation and how its well-fed prejudice
intersected with self-preservation to lead to war.

On the last day of class, the professor polled the class again,
surely expecting that bright young students at a well-regarded
university would have engaged the material in a serious manner
and come to more evolved conclusions. When he asked how
many still believed the Civil War was about something other
than slavery, a number of hands went up. Fewer than there
were months before, but not by much. He just stared at the
auditorium in disbelief and exasperation.

Of course, he might've known that a classroom of young
people, primarily raised and educated in a former Confederate state, had been learning about the past from people they
knew, loved, and certainly trusted far more than they did
some stranger behind a lectern. For a young adult to choose

to believe a photocopied article assigned by a professor who doesn't know their name over the worldview of their own parents and grandparents is a tall task. We humans have a strange way of telling ourselves the truths we want to believe. Those of us who want to engage the world with any kind of intellectual curiosity cannot be spared this reckoning. Eventually, we come face-to-face with the America we were not exposed to or have willingly avoided.

I was the same kid who'd done a report in third grade on the history of my elementary school, which had once been the all-Black high school in my hometown. In third grade I learned about segregation, about how long it took to integrate schools in Wilmington—years after the Supreme Court's mandate in *Brown v. Board of Education*. Through interactions with children in my school, I'd learned that there was friction between people who looked like me and my Black and Brown classmates, and I discovered a sense of responsibility that comes with being white that I am still working out within myself.

Intellectually, I knew what history had taught me—about slavery, about Jim Crow, about lynchings, about the civil rights movement—and I had the sense of right and wrong that we almost all have from the moment we begin to understand what is fair and unfair on the school playground. But there was, and sometimes still is, a dissonance between that intellectual knowledge and the identity formed in me as a white southern man who needed to be proud of who he is and where he came from. Perhaps this should not be as difficult as it often is, and should not take the form of bigotry, delusion, and even extremism, but it is and often does.

This dissonance is how we learn to live in denial of the racist history we all inherit, and this denial continues to have disastrous consequences, like QAnon conspiracy theories and armed insurrection in places that stand as the very foundation of democratic ideals in America. I grew up with this internal conflict: horrified by the history I was learning, but wanting to believe that the Confederate flag was a symbol of "heritage, not hate," as if the heritage of southern culture could be separated from the hate that had characterized the genocide of Black bodies. Deep down, I couldn't wish for a different outcome to that battle at Gettysburg, but I wanted to root for the people who came from where I came from. What was I wishing for by wishing my team had won? This is ultimately a clarifying question.

## WHAT IT MEANS TO BE "WHITE"

These myths are one way that we soothe ourselves and resist the truth of white supremacy's ruinous past and present. That resistance takes many forms: some of us retreat into defensiveness, insisting that white privilege is a myth, that America has long ago atoned for the wrongs of its racial past, that our Confederate ancestors were fighting for their way of life against intrusion from people who didn't understand them. Some of us opt for a slightly more progressive racial blindness, claiming not to see color, to "have Black friends," avoiding the ongoing conflicts raging in our culture around issues such as police violence, mass incarceration, and disparate public health outcomes for people of color. Still others of us grow militant about language, about learning, about conversation, but stop short of lifestyle changes that subvert systems built by racial inequity.

To progress beyond these ways of being, we need a redemptive way of understanding whiteness, which must include the pursuit of the truth about who we are, all that we are. That means acknowledging where we come from: the people, the violence, the theft, and the overt and more subtle ways we have conspired together to maintain the advantage whiteness offers.

We begin with naming our condition, confessing it before one another and before God. To do otherwise is to delude ourselves, to believe greater and greater lies and conspiracy theories crafted for the sole purpose of preserving whiteness and the violent oppression that comes with it. If we cannot be honest with ourselves, we cannot be honest with our Black and Brown neighbors. Most white people desire a more peaceable relationship between races, but they want this peace without justice, without walking the hard road of truth in which authentic relationships are grounded. We have never, collectively, confessed the truth about the utter pain and death the project of whiteness has wrought on people of color, and the spiritual havoc it has wrought on white people themselves.

Even as I write these words, political posturing is ongoing around the *New York Times'* 1619 Project and its incorporation into public school curricula. Critics argue that it creates a false narrative around the origins of the country, that a country that built its wealth with unpaid labor provided overwhelmingly by one racial group under threat of barbarous violence does not have inherent racism at work in its institutions. We are to believe that a country whose architects were owners of slaves, a country where racial prejudice was embedded in the written laws of the country for hundreds of years . . . is somehow not, by nature, a racist nation. We have made such a habit of lying to ourselves that it seems we can no longer distinguish the truth from fiction.

Many of us watched the attack on the US Capitol on January 6, 2021, with a kind of disbelief. We listened to our neighbors, to our friends, to our family members, to our elected leaders make assertions that cannot be supported with facts or evidence. "How," we wonder, "have so many people lost touch with reality? How have so many people rejected factual evidence as the burden of proof?" There was little surprise, however, from nonwhite corners of our country.

Whiteness, a lie itself, needs lies upon lies to be sustained. Science has shown us that race is a social construct, and history demonstrates that race was systematically developed as an idea; but if we do not understand why, we cannot understand ourselves. Geneticists are helping to expose the lie of racial difference with findings that ethnic groups in West Africa have more in common genetically with people in western Europe than they do with people in East Africa. The racial classifications we hold to as matters of fact break down in the face of science; and yet the myth persists, because myths often exist to explain realities that cannot otherwise be explained. In the case of white supremacy in America, the reality is radical inequality, and we do know the truth, we just cannot tell it. It is past time for us to tell the truth—to ourselves and to one another, and to stop gaslighting our Black and Brown siblings by denying a truth that anyone can see, if they have the will to look.

## WHITENESS RUNS DEEPER THAN YOU THINK

The primary focus among many white people when we begin conversations around racial prejudice is the individual—an individual's discriminatory words or actions. If racism is rooted in individual immoral actions, then of course none of us want to be implicated in it, and therefore we can only discuss it as someone else's problem. At some point following the civil rights movements of the 1950s and 1960s, individualized racial prejudice and overt racist language become socially unacceptable in circles where it had once been part of the social fabric. And since the most visible moments of the civil rights movement occurred across the Deep South, those who live in the northern United States could identify racism as a southern problem—an attitude I have experienced directly as a Southerner living in an area with a great many transplants from other parts of the country. Robin DiAngelo, in her book *White Fragility,* points out that this social taboo and regional stereotyping make it difficult for white people to do any self-examination when it comes to issues of white supremacy.[1] The more racism is compartmentalized, the less we are forced to reckon with it.

Frequently I have heard that the solution to racial prejudice is in the coming generation, who will come to have drastically different attitudes than their parents and grandparents because of the world they inhabit. For many white people who consider themselves progressive, working toward racial equality means being especially friendly to persons of color, refraining from telling or laughing at racist jokes or attitudes, and showing solidarity with the ongoing trauma Black and Brown people experience from the many manifestations of white supremacy that exist in our culture. This is, in fact, the perfect recipe for white supremacy to persist in America, because we are still viewing racism—and the solution to it—as a matter of individual behaviors.

In racial equity trainings I've attended, some of my white neighbors struggled with the idea that racism is not about individual attitudes, but about systematized, institutionalized prejudice. DiAngelo—among many, many others—defines racism as prejudice combined with power. What this means is that, in America, only white people can be racist. Anyone can hold racial prejudice, but only white people "have the collective social and institutional power and privilege over people of color."[2] This definition produced reticence in our training, because this meant that racism is a problem white people have a particular responsibility to deal with within themselves, and this is a particularly challenging truth for many of us to accept. Refusing to accept it means that systematized white supremacy persists, from generation to generation, because it is never dismantled. The Rev. Dr. Martin Luther King Jr. tried to tell us in his "Letter from Birmingham Jail" that progress does not "roll in on wheels of inevitability,"[3] but instead requires active, intentional, coordinated effort.

We are where we are today because, at least in part, we have not done this work. Half of medical students in 2016 believed that Black people feel less pain.[4] DiAngelo also cites a 2009 study in which white children were asked to allocate money to white and Black children, sometimes with adults in the room, sometimes not. The study found that the younger white children discriminated against Black children whether or not the adult was in the room, but the older ones only did so when there was no adult in the room. They'd learned that discrimination was socially unacceptable, but still repeated it when left to their own devices.[5] There are many implications here. One is that racial prejudice is certainly passed on to our children in more ways than we assume; but another, perhaps more important one is that when placed in positions of power that allow for discretion about the allocation of resources, white people are equipped to discriminate very early on. Presumably, at least some of these children will grow up to sit in places where actual resources are allocated.

This is how we arrive at what Eduardo Bonilla-Silva terms "racism without racists."[6] Racial prejudice is baked into the systems that make our society operate, like sugar in a cookie: standardized testing that affects college admissions, home valuations that affect lending practices and the accumulation of wealth, policing, prosecution and sentencing in the criminal justice system, school discipline and grading, policymaking that disadvantages Black and Brown people, environmental impacts that are far greater in places where racial minorities live. No prosecutor, school principal, mortgage broker, or politician would openly express racial prejudice, because of the social currency it would cost (though, lately, this can be debated). Yet racial disparities persist in all of these systems. Why? Because they were built with the intention of establishing and sustaining white supremacy in America. And those systems will continue to function exactly as they were intended to, as long as people of faith (and other people of goodwill) believe that all we have to do to combat racism is overcome individual prejudice.

Much of Jesus' ministry was spent helping individuals. The Samaritan woman at the well, the man possessed by a legion of demons, the blind man at Bethsaida, the paralytic lowered through the roof. His anger, his frustration, was with those who were in positions to change the systems that created their need and did nothing. There was the Roman Empire, which ruled with violence and coercion to extract what it could from the people, and then there were the powerful among Jesus' own people, who went along with oppressive systems because it enriched them and afforded them lives of relative ease. The latter were the targets of his harshest criticism. When imagining a modern equivalent, it is difficult not to see Christians in America in this light—people who, intentionally and unintentionally, have made peace with white supremacy because either it benefits us or it asks too much of us to undo it. We cannot begin to be who Christ calls us to be in the face of suffering and injustice without accepting that when he critiques the chief priests and scribes, he very well could mean us.

## WHITENESS IS ROOTED IN INADEQUACY

James Baldwin is among those who have seen whiteness in America most clearly. In 1963, in an interview with psychologist Kenneth Clark that aired on PBS, Baldwin cut to the heart of the matter, asserting that he was "not a n——, but a man," and that it was up to white people to find out why they had a need for a "race" they could use to elevate themselves in the first place. "If I'm not the n—— here and you invented him, you the white people invented him, then you've got to find out why. And the future of the country depends on that, whether or not it is able to answer that question."[7] This is precisely the correct question for white people to ask ourselves, but we have seldom reached the spiritual and emotional maturity to approach it.

What is it, in us, that is the reason we are unable to trust that we were made in the image of God and must denigrate the image of God in another? Baldwin wrote, "White people in this country will have quite enough to do in learning how to accept and love themselves and each other, and when they have achieved this—which will not be tomorrow and may very well be never—the Negro problem will no longer exist, for it will no longer be needed."[8]

It could be said that much of what white people have historically ascribed to Black people is projection. That is, what we do not understand, do not like, or are ashamed of in ourselves becomes the racialized generalizations we make against Black and Brown people. In the earliest days of this country, when Africans were brought here and sold as property, the language from European intellectuals—especially Christians—revolved around evangelizing and civilizing the African "savage." The irony, of course, is that the Europeans who migrated to the

Americas came from cultures that had engaged in tribal warfare and organized systems of violence. Christianity did (and still does) little to quell a penchant for violence; rather, followers of Jesus have worn crosses into battle. Today tourists wander the Tower of London, home to horrifying medieval torture in the place that fancied itself the world's primary exporter of culture and intellectualism. Heretics were burned at the stake in England until the early 1600s (the first Africans arrived in America in 1619). Resmaa Menakem writes that it is not difficult to understand why people felt the need to flee England: "Many of the English who colonized America had been brutalized, or had witnessed great brutality first-hand. Others were the children and grandchildren of people who had experienced such savagery in England."[9] Europeans transported African men, women, and children in the cargo holds of slave ships, packing bodies together in such inhuman and unsafe conditions that an untold number of human beings created in the image of God died and were unceremoniously buried in the Atlantic. White slave owners raped and beat Black women, but portrayed the Black male as the one whose sexual urges could not be controlled. White Southerners—little more than a hundred years ago—took picnics to and sent postcards from lynchings. Who, here, are the savages? Who is in need of the gospel, of being evangelized?

Laziness was and is another internalized racial stereotype associated with white supremacist thought and action, as exemplified in President Ronald Reagan's sensational claims about abuse of the welfare system, to suggest that women (particularly women of color, even though more white people than Black people are on welfare) were abusing the social safety net, and the suggestion that migrants to America are both "taking our jobs" and "living off government assistance." The foundations of this language are in the earliest pursuits of racial hierarchy, in our quest to make value judgments based on racial differences that are physiological but carry no moral, intellectual, or spiritual importance. Its roots run deep, and the amount of intellectual energy and scientific experimentation wasted in a search for physiological classifications of race could never be quantified.

Consider nineteenth-century American anthropologist Samuel Morton, who set out to study the size and shape of human skulls as a means of judging differences in intelligence between races. In his hierarchy of Egyptians (revered for their art, architecture, and culture), Morton prized "large crania and straight facial angles," which he regarded as Greek and most similar to the standards of beauty upheld in Greece's famous artwork. On the other end of the spectrum of Morton's Egyptian specimens were "Semitic" types, which he described as having a "comparatively receding forehead, long, arched and very prominent nose" and deserving of little respect because they had been "admitted to Egypt only upon sufferance."[10] Somehow—the amount of logical gymnastics boggles the mind—Morton concluded that Egyptians could be grouped with Greeks as evidence that white people were of superior intellect. In her book *The History of White People,* historian Nell Irvin Painter says Morton believed that "what looked like wooly hair in ancient Egyptian depictions" was actually wigs worn over their real hair, which Morton believed was straight and lighter in color like "that of the fairest Europeans of the present day."[11]

Of course, this is entirely illogical. What could motivate such (apparently) earnest failings in scientific method and understanding, in someone who had been trained and spent countless hours working at his discipline? White supremacy is a verdict in search of evidence, and Morton was only one among many who have worked at creating that evidence. Why is that evidence so important? Painter brings forward a helpful conclusion from sociologist Max Weber. Wealthy, privileged people want to believe that what they have comes from "underived, ultimate, and qualitatively distinctive *being*. . . . The fortunate man is seldom satisfied with the fact of being fortunate. Beyond this, he needs to know that he has a right to his good fortune. He wants to be convinced that he 'deserves' it, and above all, that he deserves it in comparison with others. . . . Good fortune thus wants to be 'legitimate' fortune."[12]

White people want to look around at the advantages that are overwhelmingly theirs, in all areas, and believe that these advantages can somehow be justified. Otherwise, it is clear we have not earned what we have, and in a capitalist society that prizes hard work and acquisition, that is a statement on our value as human beings. We need these myths in order to live in denial about how much of what we have should not, in a just, peaceable world, be ours in the first place. But how can we explain that, even in the face of other challenges, whiteness gives the advantage? Poor whites fare better than poor Blacks, on average. Indigenous women are far more likely to be victims of violent crime. The majority of (reported) violence against transgender or gender-nonconforming people is aimed at Black or Latinx transgender women.[13]

What are we to say about the work ethic of those whose wealth was created by the back-breaking manual labor of people with the skill and stamina to do the work of, for example, planting rice along the South Carolina coast? Did those white plantation owners earn their living honestly? Did their descendants?

Owning a home is the clearest path to building generational wealth. The equity that homeowners build over the course of their lives can be passed on to their children, absent any other accumulation of assets. But in the mid-twentieth century, Black Americans were largely excluded from this opportunity, even if they had the means. The Federal Housing Administration (FHA), which backed many loans (as it does now), rated neighborhoods for their stability, and frequently the measure of that stability was the absence of minorities. Primarily Black neighborhoods were rated as unstable, and therefore not eligible for FHA loans; the practice came to be known as "redlining" because those areas were shaded red on FHA maps.[14] Even those Black Americans who did manage to secure a path to homeownership were not able to sign mortgages but instead bought "on contract," which made it much easier for the property to be seized if the buyer encountered any financial hardship.[15] Black-owned property was frequently stolen, through legal trickery or the threat of violence, as occurred in my hometown, which I will detail later. A 2001 AP report traced 406 victims of this theft, who lost an estimated 24,000 acres of land valued in the millions.[16] Imagine how much wealth would have belonged to their descendants. Likewise, the GI Bill, which gave veterans access to low-interest loans, forced Black veterans seeking those loans to work with their local Veterans Administration office and local banks, which were often unwilling to assist them.[17] The result is that access to upward financial mobility has been denied to generations of Black Americans on the basis of skin color, and an injustice that lingers in more ways than can be counted.

My own family of origin, solidly middle class, was able to help me through college and graduate school, mainly because of modest (by the standards of my classmates) assets accumulated at the same time that Black Americans were being systematically denied this access. This is a decided privilege. Social safety-net programs like SNAP benefits and Medicaid have been labeled "entitlements" by those who believe those programs are rife with abuse by people who don't deserve them or will simply not want a job as long as they are available. "Entitlement" is a telling word. It implies that the recipient is receiving something they haven't worked for, something they don't deserve. In fact, disparate economic realities were created and have been perpetuated by white people who received from Black and Brown people in this country what was not rightfully theirs. Who has behaved as if they were "entitled" to something they didn't earn?

White Christians pray on Sunday morning about the God of grace; they speak openly about the unmerited love of Jesus that is borne out on the cross, and acknowledge that our lives do not often honor such a sacrifice. However, at the mere suggestion that something unearned, like the color of their skin, has helped them in their career, there is immediate reticence. Perhaps our language about our inadequacy in light of God's unconditional love is just that, talk; or perhaps we have internalized it, believe we are unworthy, and are out to prove that worth in other ways. The truth of the gospel is that God first loves us, first offers us grace without any assurance that we will somehow be found "worthy." We are worthy only because God has made it so. The irony is that just how unlovable we can be is never in starker relief than when we soothe our own insecurities by doing physical, economic, emotional, and spiritual violence to our siblings of color.

## WHITENESS IS ABOUT THEFT

The very idea of race as a social construct was created for just this reason, to justify the theft of land, labor, and intellectual property. Even as I write these words—and likely as you read them—we are both on stolen land. The slow and often violent erasure of Indigenous people and culture began almost from the moment white Europeans arrived on American shores and continues to this day. In the early 1800s, Native Americans signed more than forty treaties ceding land to the US government. Thomas Jefferson introduced a plan to relocate Indigenous tribes to territory west of the Mississippi, and President Andrew Jackson moved aggressively to displace Indigenous peoples from their land. In Georgia, for example, the discovery of gold made land coveted, and the state government held a lottery to give Cherokee land to whites. The Cherokee sued and won in the US Supreme Court, but Jackson mocked the decision, and it was never enforced. Five years later, even though a majority of Cherokee opposed removal, the US government signed a treaty with a small minority who feared they would eventually lose to the federal government. The Cherokee were hastily rounded up in stockades and forcibly removed over harsh terrain, while whites looted the belongings they left behind. More than four thousand people died along the journey, or nearly one in five members of the Cherokee nation. This march is commonly referred to as the Trail of Tears.

For Europeans, the economic viability of settling in America was dependent on large quantities of cheap and unpaid labor, and the collective agrarian knowledge of Indigenous peoples and the Africans the settlers enslaved to help them survive, first, and then create a working economy. White migrants arrived in America with no knowledge of the land or how to sustain themselves in a climate with which they were unfamiliar. Without the knowledge shared with them by Indigenous peoples about how to grow food and navigate the landscape, white settlers in America would likely not have survived. What is the value of that expertise, acquired over generations?

Consider the Gold Coast of South Carolina, where rice created significant wealth in cities like Charleston. Rice drove the South Carolina economy for much of the colonial period, but the first European settlers in places like Virginia and South Carolina depended on rainfall for their crops. We know of two places in the world where rice was grown submerged in water, in wetland areas, in this time period—Asia and West Africa.[18] The evolution of rice growing in South Carolina to this more productive system can be traced to the arrival of African slaves. By the early 1700s, this form of growing had overtaken rain-fed rice growing and made South Carolina a wealthier colony than those in New England and the mid-Atlantic.[19] Specifically, the labor and knowledge of Black women were instrumental in the success of rice as a crop.[20] Not only was the labor on rice plantations stolen, but so was the knowledge necessary to make growing rice profitable. Walk along the Battery in Charleston, consider its homes, hotels, restaurants, and shops, and remember that much of the wealth represented there was generated by the agricultural knowledge and the labor of West African slaves, who suffered in disease-ridden rice fields while white plantation owners were enriched by the fruit of their labor.

In 1840, cotton produced by slave labor accounted for almost 60 percent of the country's exports. Just before the Civil War, one-third of all white income in cotton-growing states was earned by slave labor.[21] Yale historian David Blight notes that slaves were the largest financial asset in the country—worth more than the country's manufacturing, railroads, and its entire productive capacity *combined*.[22] There is really no way to account for the wealth white people have stolen from Black and Brown people, and how that wealth has passed from generation to generation over time—not because it couldn't be added up, but because the amount would be difficult for us to comprehend. Two hundred and forty years of slavery would be difficult enough—the universities, government buildings, transportation systems, and generational wealth created by humans whose labor and skill were stolen while their bodies were abused. But that theft has continued, in various forms, ever since.

The town I grew up in—Wilmington, North Carolina— has a beautiful historic district along the Cape Fear River, with streets still paved with their original bricks, and scenic views of the Cape Fear Memorial Bridge and the USS *North Carolina*. Along these few blocks are bars, restaurants, shops, historic homes, and new high-rise apartment buildings that will surely attract professionals from the nearby pharmaceutical company headquarters. It was not always this way. Near the turn of the twentieth century, Wilmington was North Carolina's most diverse and integrated city, with many Black-owned businesses along those downtown streets. Its status as a port city meant the infusion of arts and culture.

In 1898, a coordinated effort by white supremacists changed the face of the city—and who profited in it—forever. The campaign was led by Colonel Alfred Waddell, a white supremacist who would later become mayor of Wilmington, and a prominent mill owner named Hugh McCrae. Before the city election of 1898, Waddell exclaimed at a rally, "Go to the polls tomorrow and if you find the negro out voting, tell him to leave the polls, and if he refuses, kill him, shoot him down in his tracks."[23] White Democrats won that election, but that wasn't enough. They burned the printing press at the *Daily Record*, the only African American newspaper in the country at the time, and then marched through predominantly Black Wilmington neighborhoods, indiscriminately murdering African American citizens. No one knows exactly how many were killed, but McCrae boasted that there were ninety dead. Some say it was more than three hundred. White men forced the few African American city officials remaining to resign their positions at gunpoint. Fourteen hundred Black citizens fled the city, while others huddled in the swamps along the Cape Fear River to avoid the gun-toting white supremacists. The pastor of one of Wilmington's largest churches (then and now) proclaimed from the pulpit, "We have taken a city. To God be the praise."[24]

What they took, along with the lives, spirit, and culture of the city, was property. White Wilmingtonians, with the help of local banks, systematically laid claim to property vacated by those who had either died in the massacre or fled Wilmington for their own safety. The result was a drastically different financial landscape. How many times has property in downtown Wilmington changed hands since then? How many millions of dollars have been passed from one generation to another, and how much opportunity did that wealth create for generations of white Wilmingtonians?

You can have a nice walk along the Wilmington riverfront now. Enjoy a beer, a good meal, meander in and out of shops . . . and you would never know just how much of it is stolen. This is the story of only one city, in one state, in America. And that is only to count the financial theft. Also stolen was any semblance of a free and fair election, the right to vote and to have that vote counted, the ability to live and thrive in one's own community.

Whiteness is about theft. The specifics of the examples I've given—the theft of intellectual property, land, resources, wealth, business, and basic human rights—are only a fraction of those that could be detailed. Many towns have a story like the one in my hometown, though perhaps not as dramatic. I have not mentioned the massacre in Tulsa, the theft of land that belonged to Mexico, or the Dakota War of 1862, which saw President Lincoln authorize the public hanging of thirty-nine Dakota men. All of these are moral transgressions. How are we to justify taking from another what does not belong to us? How do we justify the casual and often callous disregard for life itself? They cannot be justified apart from the construct of whiteness. A false racial hierarchy was the balm to soothe the cognitive dissonance that comes with doing all these things while calling them anything other than theft, genocide, and exploitation.

Whiteness allows us to believe that Indigenous peoples, because they do not have the attributes we ascribe to whiteness, are therefore not fully human and are not owed basic human rights. If their customs, spirituality, dress, music, and dance can be deemed more "uncivilized" than those of white European settlers, then the erasure of their tribal identities and decimation of their population by war and disease is evolution and sophistication, not genocide.

Likewise, according to proponents of slavery, those enslaved in America were being fed and housed and their souls were saved by confessing faith in Jesus, though it is at least debatable that any faith that excludes stories of liberation like the exodus (which was often omitted from the narrative shared with slaves) and is used to perpetuate systems of economic injustice can be called Christianity. Slavery was justifiable, its proponents said, because life under the measure of whiteness is superior to the life they might have otherwise had in "uncivilized" Africa.

Whiteness is the formation of the mental and spiritual framework necessary to attend a lynching with a picnic in hand, to loot the belongings of a family that leaves its home in terror, and, more subtly, to deny a mortgage application that might be approved for a white family. Whiteness became the norm, the standard by which all other things were and are measured. If you watch and listen to what unfolds around you, this manifests itself in our daily lives all the time: whenever a teacher or broadcaster fumbles over a name that does not suit the English-speaking tongue, then chuckles about it; whenever white artists appropriate art created by people of color for greater commercial success; and in every neighborhood where Black and Brown residents are displaced by gentrification while being paid a fraction of the money their property will one day be worth.

## WHITENESS IS A CHOICE

My maternal grandfather died before I was born. I've heard stories about what kind of man he was, the ways in which I look like him (thanks for the male pattern baldness) or have some of his traits. I wish I'd had the opportunity to know him. One thing relayed to me, in our family discussions about race in America, is the language that he would use and remarks he would make about Black and Brown people. This was always explained as a generational thing, a product of the time in which he lived. He never treated anyone differently, I was told, but he used the derogatory language that so many other people of his generation did when referring to people of color.

No doubt you have heard this as well: "That's just how things were back then. Everybody talked like that." For many of us, our attitudes and cultural sensibilities shift and evolve and mirror the environment in which we find ourselves. Few of us are immune from that kind of evolution. For my own part, I am grateful for it, though I do look back at attitudes I held and language I used and wonder why I made those choices. But consider the morals that guide your life now, the ones that govern your sense of right and wrong, how you treat others, what you believe is true about the way you should be in the world. While many might share your views, likely there are others who would argue vehemently against them. All you need to do to test the theory is share what you think about the phrase "Black lives matter" at a family reunion and watch what ensues. No matter what the prevailing cultural sensibilities might be at any given time, there are always those who push back.

The same is true about white supremacy. Building America on the idea of white supremacy was not inevitable; it was a choice, and white people opted for the politics of white supremacy in unmistakable ways, even when presented with thinkers, leaders, and activists who offered an alternative. Consider contemporaries Thomas Jefferson and Samuel Stanhope Smith, who held diverging ideas about the project of whiteness and slavery. Jefferson was a slave owner, repeatedly raped the enslaved Sally Hemings (who, regardless of what stories are told, would have had no choice of whether to consent), and fathered seven children by her. Jefferson's own writings about slavery are contradictory. He wrote that slavery had a negative impact on white people, mainly due to the way it exposed the children of slave owners to violence; this would, he reasoned, "coarsen" their character.[25] Of course Jefferson wrote more widely about the inferiority of Black people, degraded their appearance, and suggested that they were best fit to be slaves.[26] But that's how all men thought in those days, right?

Well, not exactly. Samuel Stanhope Smith—while certainly not a hero of racial justice—offered some clear alternatives to Jefferson's way of thinking. Smith suggested that ideals of beauty are culturally determined, not universal, which implies that nothing about the appearance of Black people is inferior unless one has already determined that whiteness is to be desired. When Jefferson criticized the poetry of Phillis Wheatley, enslaved in Boston, and asserted that it was proof that Black people were incapable of displaying genius (the irony being that almost every distinctly American art form derived from Black culture), Smith replied that "genius requires freedom," and pointed out that none of the South's plantation owners could have matched Wheatley's skill.[27] One can hardly call Smith a revolutionary thinker by today's standards, but his way of thinking was, in some ways, an opposition to Jefferson. Likely you knew only one of their names before reading this, which tells you something about whose way of thinking gained more traction among white Americans.

This is a small example of ways we have chosen the path of white supremacy even when faced with alternative ways of thinking. When there was slavery, there were those working for abolition; when Japanese Americans were confined to internment camps, there were those advocating for their release; when four North Carolina A&T students sat down at a lunch counter in Greensboro and refused to leave, there were some who supported them amid the threats and insults hurled their way. To say, then, that this is just "how things were" is not entirely accurate. When Jesus and Barabbas were presented before the crowds outside Pilate's chambers and the crowds were asked who should be released, the overwhelming response was "Barabbas!" Maybe that's how things were, but they still had a choice.

For white privilege to continue to exist—for white people to be afforded certain privileges and opportunities, or be spared certain realities, because of the color of their skin—each of us has to make a choice. While we may not have created this privilege for ourselves, we do choose whether or not we sustain it, in small and large ways. Perhaps we are inclined to accept the poor choices of our ancestors because we do not want to be held accountable for going along with prevailing winds of our own time. But we could choose to change our patterns of living in the interest of justice, so that our children do not have to look at what we did or did not do and think, "That's just how things were."

## WHITENESS IS SELF-HARM

Whiteness has held untold material benefit for white people, for our ancestors and our heirs, but it is spiritual death. We have been taught (consciously or unconsciously) that segregated lives are safe, secure lives—in our schools, in our neighborhoods, in our workplaces. We are not taught to question what this segregation of our lives may have cost us.[28] The way of Jesus orients us around community, around belonging to one another. The foundational story of the church, Pentecost, teaches us that one of the great gifts of belonging to the church and receiving the Holy Spirit is finding common understanding among different people. Those first Christians lived in intentional community, where they held all things in common, where those who had much did not have too much and those who had little did not have too little. It was a community so committed to the well-being of the whole that when Ananias and Sapphira withheld property that might have benefited everyone, they were struck dead.

Whiteness prevents this kind of mutuality. It defines difference in a way that rejects the beauty of diversity and lends itself to exploitation. It is the lie that prevents us from seeing the beauty and the wisdom in cultures that wear less (or different) clothing, or play different instruments, or speak in languages that do not suit our own ears. How much genius, how much beauty, how much insight into the adventure of human existence have we missed because we have clung to the lie that whiteness is prescriptive, the true mark of worthiness? In the process of stealing from others, we have stolen from ourselves.

It has also led to the creation of more wealth and more power than can be held in any faithful way. In the Gospels, wealth and power are often obstacles to those who wish to take up the way of Jesus. It would be easier, Jesus said, for a camel to go through the eye of a needle than for a rich man to enter the kin-dom of heaven (Mark 10:25). What, then, are we to think of those who have not only acquired the wealth that comes with empire, but done so at the expense of the humanity of others created in the image of God? And what is required of those whose identity has been formed—and elevated—through the subjugation of others? These are the fundamental questions we must answer, and to which we now turn.

# 5

## *Shedding Whiteness*

No one alive today is responsible for the creation of a culture (including a justice system, an economy, and an education system) built on white supremacy. White supremacy is a lie we have inherited, and the fruits of it are injustices passed down to us. While we did not create it, we have inherited the legacy of white supremacy and our lives have benefited from it in extravagant ways. It is no surprise, then, that in the face of increasing racial and religious diversity in America that threatens the stronghold of white political and economic power, we have seen the reemergence of white supremacists looking to maintain and reestablish attitudes about race that were once socially unacceptable in many circles. What looks like hate and the reassertion of white dominance is rooted in fear: fear of losing long-held advantages, fear of cultural change that shifts social norms, fear of accountability for past wrongs and the present status quo, fear of what exactly we will be if we are not all the things associated with whiteness. What would our lives look like without the inherent advantages that come with being white in America?

We who live inside the bubble of whiteness, especially white maleness, know that these attitudes, and the actions that accompany them, have always been an open secret and that the preservation of whiteness remains near to the heart of those who hold power in our communities and in our nation. Large swaths of our families, our churches, our government, our industries, have no interest in acknowledging that whiteness as currently understood needs to be reframed—not only for the restoration of justice in our country, but also for the freedom of our own souls. Even those who do acknowledge it often do so in ways that don't offer substantive change, soothing the symptoms of white supremacy without addressing the disease itself.

Recently, a performative form of racial awareness has taken hold in our popular culture. We see social media campaigns, book clubs, and corporate advertisements that send messages aimed at reconciliation and inclusivity but have minimal impact in a practical sense. Perhaps the popular narrative shifts, but much more than that is necessary to undo the entrenched white supremacy in America. After the murder of George Floyd in 2020, I noticed a number of friends on social media "blacking out" the profile pictures on their social media accounts. This is a fine act of solidarity and does make a public statement about one's values, but this is a ripple in the ocean of systemic racism. Instead, maybe the sadness and anger we feel could be converted to fuel for a life aimed at deconstructing white supremacy, if we were willing to sit with it long enough.

There are now and always have been those who have lived as allies and stood in opposition to the terror of slavery, of Jim Crow, of segregation, and who are working now to stop the school-to-prison pipeline and end mass incarceration. They are doing the hard and gritty work of struggling against racialized inequality. I want to suggest that those of us who have thrown up our hands or simply moved forward with our lives, despite gaining knowledge of the pervasive violence and oppression carried out by white people (laid out in the previous chapter) that has shaped and continues to shape the world we live in today, can no longer live lives of neutrality. "To be neutral in a situation of injustice," Archbishop Desmond Tutu said, "is to have chosen sides already. It is to support the status quo."[1] Martin Luther King, writing from a jail cell in Birmingham, took the white moderates to task, arguing that they were a greater threat to the struggle for equal rights for Black Americans than those who were actively opposed. "Shallow understanding from people of goodwill is much more frustrating than absolute misunderstanding from people of ill will. Lukewarm acceptance is much more bewildering than outright rejection."[2] Some fifty-six years after he wrote those words, it is time for those who have lived under the lie of whiteness, this author included, to begin deconstructing the house that was built to shelter us. It is no longer enough to be "not racist"; America needs the people who call themselves white to be committed to the work of dismantling white supremacy within ourselves and in our institutions.

In a real sense, it is nearly impossible to confess the deeply toxic nature of white identity, both in our history and in our present American reality, without offering some redemptive way to think, act, and live in the aftermath of such a confession. Many white responses to conversations around racial justice, especially those that result in defensiveness, shame, or worse—more deeply entrenched racist ideals—are rooted in this apparent void. Having deconstructed a particular worldview, we must go about the work of reconstructing an alternative in its place, or there will only ever be resistance where there might have been real transformation. No human being, regardless of how culpable they may be in the suffering and oppression of others, willingly leaves behind a worldview without the articulation of one found to be more appealing. We have not grasped the mystery of what Jesus meant when he said that those who are willing to lose their lives will find them.

## FREEING OURSELVES FROM WHITENESS

Our conversations around race in many white circles, even (or especially) in "liberal" circles, have lacked the imagination necessary to connect the deconstruction of unjust systems to the salvation of God. Jesus does this frequently—he links relinquishing privilege with following him, creating a more just world he calls the kin-dom of God. The cost is often great, but this is the way Jesus saves us, the way Jesus loves us. This means that unlearning white supremacy is not just about honoring the lives of Black and Brown people and creating a more just world, but also about the liberation and salvation of white people. The former should be enough reason to unlearn old habits and seek out new ones but if not, perhaps the latter might be. While our racial history exists in America because institutional racism has afforded real and tangible benefit to white Americans, it has also brought about a kind of spiritual death when viewed in light of the gospel.

In our privilege, we are alienated from one another. In our privilege, we are propped up by systems of inequality. In our privilege, we learn habits and develop sensibilities that are so deeply ingrained in us that by the time we are aware of a need for inner transformation and outward advocacy to effect social change, we also realize it will take the rest of our lives to work through the way whiteness has formed our identities. Our privilege separates us from our neighbors, makes us oblivious to the truth of our own lives, disconnects us from the land we occupy—and, for followers of Jesus, fills us with the kind of spiritual blindness Jesus called his disciples to overcome. This is not so much a privilege.

The church seems to be uniquely equipped to form the imagination of a new way of life. We are stewards of the scriptural story, which demonstrates both humanity's capacity for creating systems that marginalize a particular group of people and also God's deliberate and insistent intervention in human history to tear down those systems. Without forming new habits, we resort to old ones. To leave behind white supremacy is to leave behind a particular kind of occupation of the mind and heart and body, in search of liberation from the way white supremacy entraps the moral, spiritual self and makes us complicit in a system that does harm to the land and to Black and Brown bodies. However, without a destination on the horizon, we soon long for the familiarity of this spiritual bondage rather than the strange land of promise that God has in store. To that end, my hope for this chapter is to draw on the spiritual imagination inherent in my faith tradition to articulate what a journey away from the lie of white supremacy may look like. This is, of course, not an exhaustive description, but a place to begin.

## LET GO OF GUILT

This place of paralysis, in my experience, is where most white people stay. Confronted with the legacy of terror bound up in white supremacy, white people tend to feel both helpless and guilty in the face of grand acts of violence and injustice that cannot be undone. On a recent visit to the National Museum of African American History and Culture, I arrived at the end of the four-hundred-year journey, having viewed Emmett Till's casket, seen depictions of bodies crammed into slave ships, read the testimonies of mothers who had watched their children sold like livestock on the auction block. All of this evil was carried out by people who look like me. What was I to do with my feelings of helplessness and grief, my doubt that we could ever be liberated from the sins of our past? Surely grief and sadness are appropriate responses to those atrocities, but when they become guilt, the possibility of real transformation is limited. Guilt is not the healthiest emotion, and it can also be primarily self-centered. When confronted with the suffering of another, being brought to a place of guilt for one's part can be fine and healthy; to stay in a place of guilt, however, is to begin to make the encounter about your own experience and not about the experience of those who have suffered.

Beyond that, we often tend to rebel against guilt eventually, in defense of the ego. There is something fundamentally wrong when we are more concerned about being called "racist" than we are about whether our actions have caused others harm or if we are complicit in systems of racial oppression. Ultimately, this is not about us. This is about transforming American culture and our place in it. We must do the work necessary to move past our sensitivity to the notion that we might be accountable for broad systems of oppression that, though they may not have been constructed by us individually, were built and are maintained on our behalf.

"When white people stop short of reconciliation, it's often because they are motivated by a deep need to believe in their own goodness, and for that goodness to be affirmed over and over and over again," writes Austin Channing Brown in *I'm Still Here: Black Dignity in a World Made for Whiteness*. "But reconciliation is not about white feelings. It's about diverting power and attention to the oppressed, toward the powerless."[3]

Consider the flood of videos depicting police brutality, including the murder of George Floyd. For white moderates, who lived with a blindness about the daily experience of Black Americans, these videos have served as a kind of awakening, the same way images of Bull Connor's dogs and fire hoses did at the height of the civil rights movement. They shock the conscience, and all of the emotions that come with that experience are necessary. The moment we fail to be shocked and grieved by images of violence, by the senseless loss of life, is the moment when we no longer possess the moral center that comes with believing that we are all created in the image of God. Imagine, however, how the tears and sadness of white people who are just now coming to these emotions must sound to Black and Brown Americans who have lived with this ongoing trauma their whole lives. Imagine how tiresome it must be to see tears and sadness that are not accompanied with any meaningful form of allyship, advocating for change that might address the source of those tears in the first place. Imagine what it is like to sit in book groups and racial reconciliation groups where white emotions demand center stage, where Black and Brown people are asked to manage our inability to regulate our emotions in the interest of pursuing substantive transformation.

There are places for our emotions. We should do the work of moving through them and seek out the right kind of help managing them. But eventually, we have to get over ourselves. White Americans resist the demonization of their skin color (a rich irony, surely), but there is nothing inherently wrong with having European American ancestry. Ruby Sales argues that it is "how you actualize that history and how you actualize that reality" that makes the difference. People of color do not need our guilt. They need our investment in moving America beyond its racialized past and present.[4] Shame and guilt around whiteness serve no purpose—in fact, they only lead to more harm—if we do not learn to actualize living in bodies with white skin in different, more restorative ways in our own lives.

## KNOW YOUR HISTORY (AND STOP ROMANTICIZING IT)

In the previous chapter, I told the story of my hometown, Wilmington, North Carolina, and the violent coup of 1898 that resulted in the theft of property and the basic rights that come with living in a democracy, as well as terrible suffering. When I learned this history, I was angry that it took me until my midtwenties to learn it in detail. I was frustrated with my education and the narrative present in my hometown, but at a certain point those who claim to believe in the work of justice bear responsibility for understanding the lives their neighbors live and looking around at the place we inhabit and asking fundamental questions about what kind of place it is for the people who live there—especially the marginalized—and how it got that way. Chances are, some racial trauma has shaped the place where you live, or a racialized pattern of mortgage lending, zoning, public utilities, or the like has disproportionately affected people of color there.

No one in power has much motivation to make sure these stories are told. This is why the fight over who writes our history and what kind of history we teach is so fierce, why many white people do not want young people learning critical race theory or understanding how our institutions came to be so racialized. The narrative of our life together matters. We read the Bible for this very reason. We believe that by hearing the stories of how our ancestors in faith discerned the presence of God in their lives, how God showed up to them in people and in places that liberated them from the circumstances that held them captive, how God held powerful people to account for creating unjust systems, we will learn to see God at work in our own lives, in the world still filled with so much pain. Why else would slaveholders carefully omit the story of the exodus, if history did not have the power to give life to our present? If we begin to understand how race motivated the formation of our institutions, how it shaped our communities, then we begin to see our present with greater clarity. If there are those who wish those stories not be told, we should always ask why—and allow their resistance to deepen our determination and our curiosity.

Because these histories are actively obscured, you will have to learn and elevate them for yourself, and you will almost certainly not be able to rely on the predominant white accounts of the story that has helped to shape the place that shapes you. In the work my congregation has done around racial justice with partners in our community, we learned that our neighbors in southeast Raleigh, where Black people had been exiled during segregation, were pushed into a swamp where the city had once dumped its raw sewage. As a result, the area continues to flood when nearby Walnut Creek floods. Continued development along the watershed—even in our area, miles from southeast Raleigh—affects runoff and the likelihood of flooding in those areas. No one was going to tell us this, unless we took the time to listen and find out for ourselves. This history is relevant to planned development. How development is done in our community and what kind of runoff it creates affects our neighbors downstream, who live in our watershed. What would seem like development that could be good for the community takes on a different tenor when viewed in light of how our history shapes our present.

I also grew up in a place that romanticized the Confederacy. Almost every town has a monument to the Confederacy; not so much an acknowledgment of or a structural confession to its history of institutionalized prejudice and the terror of slavery, but a monument to simpler times—as if there were an era in American history not stained with the blood of Black bodies, marred by indifference to human suffering. It is difficult to believe we will be transformed, or that we will be part of the transformation, if we lack the courage and moral fortitude to tell the truth.

The Confederacy was aimed at dismantling the United States of America. Whenever American flags and Confederate flags are flown together as some kind of patriotic expression, the flags flown are actually those of enemy armies. While the depth of that kind of cognitive dissonance surely has many explanations, it is due in part to our inability to describe our history accurately.

Every time we absorb a whitewashed story of racial reconciliation in a movie, or celebrate the virtues of those who founded this country without also acknowledging the deep contradictions inherent in their belief that owning other human beings could be justified, we communicate something about our relationship with the truth, and how much we are willing to see and acknowledge our neighbors. There is irony in the notion that men are taught that a key element of masculinity is being responsible and protective, but we resist the notion that we are responsible for the legacy we have inherited. There is irony in the notion of "cancel culture" when so much of our history was intentionally and actively erased.

I cannot overstate the healing power I have seen unleashed when I have simply been willing to name truths that people who look like me have been unwilling to tell. It is not complicated. We just need to tell the truth. Our neighbors carry the trauma of this past in their bodies; when we gloss over or romanticize it, it takes hold in new ways. We must tell these truths—especially the hard ones, the ones that grieve us. Only the truth can set us free.

## GRIEF WILL BE PART OF THE EQUATION

When we learn our history, likely we will also learn that our teachers didn't tell us the full truth, that our parents and grandparents held or hold attitudes that are problematic, that we have used offensive language, laughed at hurtful jokes, and—more significantly—been the beneficiary of a system tilted in our favor. Rightly, there is grief to feel upon these kinds of realizations, but the grief cannot be a deterrent to doing the work. I remember, at an early age, feeling grief when those around me slipped into racial stereotyping that was problematic, if not intentionally harmful. I remember feeling that grief in the times I realized that those things had slipped from my own mouth. I remember the shame of learning that I had relatives with Klan robes in their closets. Most white Americans can confess to some of the above. The difficulty in confession is not in acknowledging a history to which we have no connection, but in acknowledging that people we love dearly did not tell us the whole truth or held racial attitudes that cannot be excused.

By now the "stages" of grief are part of our collective consciousness. We know that there is denial, that there is anger, that there is bargaining, depression, and perhaps eventually acceptance, and that these do not occur in any linear way, but in a swirl that is often difficult to manage. We can identify all of these stages in the grief of realizing our own complicity and that of our ancestors, since it shapes many of the clichéd responses we bring out in discussions on race. "None of my ancestors owned slaves" and "My grandfather used racist language but always treated people well" sound like denial. "At some point we just have to move on" and the tokenism of boardrooms, classrooms, and publications look and sound like bargaining. The emotional defense of Confederate monuments, the resolute defense of law enforcement in the face of continued violence against unarmed Black and Brown Americans, and the downright obstructionism faced by Barack Obama as president all look and sound a lot like anger about what we stand to lose—our myths and our affection for them. This grief is often a by-product of our binaries. We like to be able to sort people into "good" or "bad" when it comes to their racial attitudes, as if we cannot love imperfect people, as if the people we have venerated are not also capable of having moral failures. You hold both things within yourself all the time—the person who desires to be transformed, to grow in grace and love and to become a greater partner with God in the remaking of the world, *and* the person with ingrained prejudice who, to return to Paul's words, continues to do what you do not want to do and not do what it is you know you should (Rom. 7:15–20). You are not just one of the other. Neither are the people you most want to defend. We have trouble telling the truth about the architects of the US government, who wrote beautifully eloquent words that tell a deep truth, because we cannot hold together the reality that they were also virulent racists who did not believe that the words they wrote applied to everyone. Both things can be true, but it requires tolerating more nuance and complexity than we would like.

Moses was both a murderer and a leader of liberation. Paul was an oppressor of God's people who carried that history into a life disrupted by God. Yes, these are people whose faith is an integral part of our scriptural story, but their failures are too; the fact that these elements of their stories are included means that we can believe in God's power to redeem and still tell the whole story, even the ugly parts. It invites us to tell the truth, and if we can tell the truth, there will be no more illusions for us to grieve when they inevitably disappear.

We will not move beyond the status quo of racial injustice in America without white people facing this grief in a healthier and more productive way. "People who cannot suffer," James Baldwin wrote, "can never grow up, can never discover who they are."[5] There is just no way around the confrontation that will come when recognizing the betrayals that are part of one's own history. White folks need to summon the communal resources to name this grief for what it is and to work through it ourselves without heaping more harm on people of color. Again, the church is uniquely equipped for this work.

I suspect that Peter, in the courtyard of the high priest, had an experience of grief we can scarcely imagine when the cock crowed in the distance. He had let Jesus down. When the risen Jesus appeared to him on the beach, and asked three times if Peter loved him, he still did not understand why Jesus might have reason to wonder if he truly understood the question and was prepared to give a meaningful answer. And yet Peter eventually rose from grief to become a living witness to the redeeming and reconciling power of God. For this to take place, Peter did not—he could not have—become a prisoner to the grief that came with his own failures.

## SHUT UP AND LISTEN

One thing I have learned from paying attention to my own spirit and to the behavior of my peers in the midst of difficult conversations around race (or gender, for that matter, which is why this instruction is uniform across the sections of this book) is that listening is profoundly difficult. This is because those of us who have been socialized as white males have learned to take for granted that our voices not only will be heard but also are needed. Generally, we have no hesitancy in speaking responsively and authoritatively or asserting ourselves in the midst of the conversation. Moreover, we tend to move to the front of the conversation, framing it from our viewpoint, no matter our conversation partners.

I have a friend who owned retired racing greyhounds. When she went running with her running club and took the dogs, the dogs were going to the front of the pack, no questions asked. This is what they were bred for, what they were trained to do. More and more I notice how often we assume white male leadership in all conversations. When we find ourselves in places where decisions are being made, laws are being passed, or debates are being held, we stride toward the front of the conversation, as if our viewpoint is primary, as if it must be heard. A Bible commentary publishes the writing of four male scholars on a passage describing one of the first female disciples. Legislation disproportionately affecting women or minorities is passed by large rooms of white men. This, we assume, is our birthright.

This is our inheritance as well: to go to the front; to doubt that Black people have anything to teach us, not only about ourselves, but also about the world. But we cannot know ourselves fully without the truth Black Americans have to tell us about who we are. As we enter into spaces of conversation, we are called to resist the urge to speak, to respond, and most of all to determine the boundaries of the conversation. By pursuing this healthy, restrained approach, we can have just relationships, free of power and domination.[6]

Jonathan Wilson-Hartgrove draws on the Benedictine practices of listening, staying put, and constantly reforming your life in the context of learning to understand your own whiteness, in the light of the experience of your Black and Brown neighbors. "'Just shut up and listen' might be the most important instruction for anyone committed to unlearning whiteness."[7] I invite you to pay attention to your emotions as you read it put that plainly and bluntly. I know so many white men who bristle at the idea that they must be quiet while others voice their suffering and express difficult truths about how white men, particularly, have hurt them. We do not know how to handle the notion that our perspective is not primary or vital to the conversation. And because of that bristling, we never learn to listen intently, actively, without simultaneously formulating a response or deciding what we must do differently, which is not really listening.

I do an active listening exercise with every couple who see me for premarital counseling. The task of the listener is to repeat, as close to word-for-word as they can, what the other said—without interpretation, translation, or argument. It is virtually impossible to be successful at the task if you are not completely focused on the one who is communicating. This is the kind of listening white men are called to practice around Black and Brown people who have deep truths to teach us about who we are, about the country we live in, about the God we serve. Be quiet, for once, and listen. Listen without formulating your response, without crafting a rebuttal, which more often than not will be fashioned to guard your own ego. Without this practice, you cannot really hear.

A fine line is crossed, however, when we rely on Black and Brown people to educate us. *We must resist asking Black and Brown people, living with the trauma of white supremacy, to be our teachers.* It may be that our Black and Brown neighbors are willing to share their experience of carrying this identity in a country shaped by white supremacy, but the purpose of these relationships cannot be resolving the questions we need to have answered. As a student, I've never walked into a classroom on the first day of class and insisted I dictate the curriculum. We also run the risk of turning neighbors who might be friends into tokens instead, asking them to speak for all people everywhere who look like them, a pressure none of us wants.

The reality is that there are plenty of ways to learn, to educate yourself on the dynamics of race in America without burdening the closest person of color you know with the responsibility. Truly, a library card and a Netflix account are as good a starting place as any. If you have not read James Baldwin or James Cone or Malcolm X, searched for William Barber or Bryan Stevenson on YouTube, visited an African American museum or art exhibit, how can you justify asking someone to turn their own trauma into your Cliff's Notes on race in America? If the work is important—and I hope I have shown that it is—you must do it without shortcuts.

Of course, listening is not an end unto itself, as even those who do it best have often apparently believed. "Too often," Austin Channing Brown writes, "dialogue functions as a stall tactic, allowing white people to believe they've done something heroic when the real work is yet to come."[8] The number of panel discussions, special worship services, book clubs, workshops, and trainings you attend means little if the act of listening does not fundamentally change your worldview, and change it in such a way that necessitates a change in how you live, how you act, how you vote, where and how and whether you show up and act on behalf of the marginalized when the question of racial justice is at stake in your community, in your state, in our nation—even in your church.

## DROP THE REQUIREMENT FOR ASSIMILATION

There is almost no circle of American life where white cultural preferences are not the prescribed norm—from standards of beauty to hairstyles to language to the structures of organizations, including churches. In the congregation I serve in North Carolina, many of the newer members of our community are people of color. While this has been wonderful, it has confronted us with deep questions about how power is held and how we as a community can create space for those who come to bring the fullness of who they are to our communal worship, education, and administration, without requiring that they assimilate to our white suburban norms around those communal practices. The continued segregation of the church owes largely to the unwillingness of those in predominantly white spaces to relinquish the (spoken or unspoken) requirement that anyone who wishes to belong relinquish the unique experience of their own Blackness. Both inside and outside the church, people of color are often required to code-switch—to speak and act in ways that ensure their acceptance and ultimate success within white systems. This is not only oppressive; it is muting the human experience. When we require assimilation to certain standards of dress, ways of speaking, modes of expression, or styles of leading, our communities lose, because we lose the richness that comes with each person living fully into who God made them to be.

In Acts, the church is continually pushed to define the margins of belonging and forced to reckon with the consequences of welcoming those who receive the gift of the good news of Jesus crucified and risen from the dead. Luke frames this as the work of the Spirit—it is not that the early Christian community shapes its identity around a need for cultural relevance or tries to be as permissive as the culture, but the Spirit intervenes and brings about these encounters that redraw communal boundaries, because this is apparently the agenda God has for the growth of this movement. Jesus spent time with sinners and tax collectors and Samaritans and women; then his disciples continue this outward movement. In each of these stories, a fundamental transformation takes place, not only for those who receive the good news of Jesus of Nazareth, but also for those who are called to share it. Each of them must wrestle with how this shift in trajectory changes them, and the Christian community must wrestle with how welcoming people from different backgrounds and different cultures changes the nature of the community to which they belong. It is difficult work, but it is apparently the work the Spirit has in mind.

Fundamentally, this changes the identity of the community and the norms by which it operates; this change is one you and I might be grateful for, since we are grafted into this story by virtue of these ever-expanding boundaries. If these encounters changed those communities and led them to deep discernment and confrontation about what values are essential in a community centered on the love and grace of God revealed in Christ Jesus, how much more might our racial awareness lead us to discernment and confrontation about what values we have made essential for belonging in our communities? Which of these standards are rooted not in the Word of God, but in the doctrine of white supremacy?

## YOUR INTENTIONS DON'T MATTER

The impact of your lifestyle, what you say (or don't) in important moments, how you choose to act within the systems traditionally used to oppress people of color, and how you show up as an ally in critical moments that may not affect you directly are far more important than what you feel. Most of us stop believing the term "racism" applies to us when we have examined the attitudes we hold and decide we are not going to let those attitudes affect how we treat other people. But racism is far more pernicious than that. Given the way we have been conditioned in our racialized society, we likely still commit microaggressions (small interactions that reinforce negative or dehumanizing dynamics that exist for certain populations), make statements that are ignorant or offensive, or stay silent when our voice might have made a difference. These happen all the time without our knowing—and despite our best intentions. Typically, we judge ourselves based on our intentions and judge others based on their actions.

Ultimately, we are accountable for the version of ourselves we present to the world, including the harm we inevitably do from the deeply embedded prejudices we acquire in a racialized culture like America's. When what we say or what we do does harm, we must accept that this is part of who we have been, even as we acknowledge that it is not who we hope to be in the future. The carefully crafted apologies made by TV personalities and politicians almost always include the words "this does not reflect who I am or the values I hold" before they are sent off to sensitivity training, presumably to understand why what they said was wrong. In part, we create who we are by what we do. As long as I believe that I do not have a problem if I do not intend harm, no sensitivity or equity training will help me live differently. Jesus, in a debate about what defiles a person, argued that it isn't what goes in (unclean food) but what comes out that defiles a person (Matt. 15:10–20). If what comes forth from the inmost part of who we are does harm, then this is the reality we must face, so that we can be reconciled to ourselves, God, and one another.

We face decisions all the time that place our intentions and the consequences of our actions in sharp relief. What are the criteria by which we choose to buy a home? If it's because there are "good schools," are those schools considered "good" because they are racially homogeneous? Or, if it's because it's in a "good neighborhood," what do we mean when we say that? When we become parents, do we advocate that the school district lines be drawn to benefit our own children, or to benefit all children, especially those who have historically done without the resources others of us have enjoyed? Do we shop in stores we're used to, or seek out minority-owned businesses? All of these decisions can be made from a place of self-interest without any "intent" to hurt anyone else or to keep established patterns going. But if your decisions do harm, how much does what you intended matter to the person—or people—on the other end?

## REPAIR THE BREACH

I encounter white people all the time who find the idea of reparations untenable, who believe affirmative action is no longer necessary. I tell them to imagine digging a pit with a shovel for four hundred years—how deep and wide and expansive it would be—and then filling in the hole with a shovel for forty or so years and expecting it to be filled. America has done little to correct the economic disenfranchisement, the generations of emotional and physical abuse and trauma, and the terror of living daily in an environment where one's body is never safe from violation or harm. In many cases, as we have seen, what we have called progress—refilling the hole—has actually been continued digging, only with a different instrument.

What would it take to fill this hole? Doubtless it would take white people relinquishing assets acquired over time. There is certainly biblical precedent for that. Zacchaeus—the man who climbed a tree to watch Jesus from a safe distance—was a tax collector. Tax collectors were hated because they took what the government commanded, plus a little more on top of it to line their own pockets. When Jesus invited himself into Zacchaeus's home, Zacchaeus was converted. His conversion, however, was not complete until he was prepared to make reparations. Zacchaeus said, "'Look, half of my possessions, Lord, I will give to the poor; and if I have defrauded anyone of anything, I will pay back four times as much'" (Luke 19:8). It was then that Jesus pronounced that salvation had come to Zacchaeus's home. If there was fear, if there was grief, if there was reluctance on Zacchaeus's part, it is not relayed by the Gospel writer; however, it is not hard to imagine that all those may have been present. Zacchaeus was promising to relinquish some of the comfort he'd acquired, some of the things that made his life demonstrably better, easier.

In our culture, building just communities will take sacrifice, though sacrifice is not exactly the proper term for returning something that wasn't yours to begin with—the labor, the property, the wealth that were stolen over generations do not rightfully belong to white America. White Americans will need to accept that it can and should cost us something, maybe a lot—but that the cost isn't so much a cost when it is deconstructing a system that has made us spiritually unwell, an obstruction to our discipleship. We think we want advantages for our children, well-resourced schools that will help them get ahead of their neighbors, instead of well-integrated schools where our children learn to be better global citizens by having relationships with people who have different experiences of the world. We think we benefit from law enforcement assuming our innocence because of the color of our skin, even though this creates a simmering fear and anger in our community that occasionally boils over. What feels like good news in the short run is keeping us from being the kind of communities we would really value. There will be no postracial America until and unless lingering inequalities from America's formation as a racialized culture are addressed. The challenge is weaning ourselves off the addictive nature of white supremacy in favor of the kind of values that characterize what Jesus calls the kin-dom of God.

It is possible the hole we dug together can't be filled, but as Ta-Nehisi Coates writes in "The Case for Reparations," the answer to the question of reparations may not be as important as a collective conversation about the question itself:

> An America that asks what it owes its most vulnerable citizens is improved and humane. An America that looks away is ignoring not just the sins of the past but the sins of the present and the certain sins of the future. More important than any single check cut to any African American, the payment of reparations would represent America's maturation out of the childhood myth of its innocence into a wisdom worthy of its founders.[9]

## USE YOUR PLACE

Anyone over eighteen reading this likely has the right to vote. As a voter, you can consider not only what serves your own self-interest, but also what serves the interest of your neighbors of color, including working to oppose voter suppression tactics often aimed at minority communities. Imagine, in discerning whom you might vote for, if you considered not only whom you favor, but how people of color feel about your preferred candidate. Does this candidate advocate for racial justice? Are they attentive to the needs of minority communities? How might it hold politicians accountable if there were a portion of white voters whose votes were won by that candidate's appeal to minority voters? Each of us has this power, inherent in our democracy, and the gift of discernment in how we use it.

There are very few vocations one can hold in America that distance you from the work of racial justice. Certainly, this is true for those employed in pastoral ministry—we have the responsibility to hold the life, death, and resurrection of Jesus up against the systems of sin and injustice that entrap our own people and those in our community, and the sin of systemic racism surely counts among them. While this may seem obvious, challenging predominantly white congregations who pay our salaries with uncomfortable news about racial injustice is not in the comfort zone of most mainline preachers. If it were, most of what has been written here would have already been said to vast swaths of Americans decades ago, when there still was a churchgoing plurality in our culture. The work is no less urgent, no less germane to the call of the pastor and preacher than it was in what we commonly think of as more racially turbulent times. We pastors ultimately bear great responsibility for the spiritual well-being of those in our care. If we visited our cardiologist in a cold sweat, with chest pains and an elevated blood pressure, and our physician did not treat our symptoms with the urgency they demanded, this would amount to malpractice. What do we call it when we know that the symptoms of white supremacy are present in our congregation but do not treat them with the urgency they deserve?

Imagine if those who work in the lending industry, or in real estate, took on the task of working for racial justice in their vocations. Or those who work in public education, who are often witness to and swept up in patterns of inequality. What of administrators and school board members who have a choice between working toward what creates a more just education system and what benefits the loud minority who seek advantages for their own children only? Medical professionals are proximate to this work, given the vastly different outcomes reported for people of color, especially women of color, in medical treatment.[10] What would happen if part of being a medical professional was working for racial equity in how patients are diagnosed and treated, and how medical research is conducted? Those who work in the business world, human resources, and all levels of government are near to the decision-making processes that have traditionally excluded and marginalized people of color.

Raising issues related to racial justice may be unpopular or cause difficulty in one's career or work environment, but it is certainly what is necessary for these well-oiled systems to be reprogrammed. Systemic injustice is ingrained in systems, yes, but these systems are made up of people. Law enforcement officers, lawyers, judges, and lawmakers all have a hand in the criminal justice system, how it works and doesn't work.

Engineers and architects who design buildings, roads, and infrastructure can consider not only the environmental impacts of their work, but how their work may disparately impact communities of color. These are not strangers, they are our neighbors. They might be you.

In an interview with journalist and radio host Krista Tippett, Ruby Sales pointed to the apparent lack of voices articulating a redemptive theology of whiteness. "It's almost like white people don't believe that other white people are worthy of being redeemed."[11] As is the case with much of what Ruby Sales observes, past and present, she is right. I suspect that the way we have become paralyzed in the face of the machine of institutionalized racism we feel helpless to stop, the way we have transformed our feelings of guilt and shame into anger and resistance to the work of justice, the way we vacillate between defensiveness and compassion, all owe largely to our deep-seated doubt about whether we (and our society) can be redeemed. I will not argue that this doubt is logically well founded. But the gospel is not logical. Jesus offered paths forward and roads to redemption to those who had long ago forfeited any right to such.

Each of us reaches a moment of decision when offered grace—will we accept this opportunity for repentance and redemption, or is the muscle memory of sin and injustice too much for us to overcome? There is a path to a redemptive life lived out in white skin. The question simply is whether we will lean into the hard work that life requires or retreat into the same patterns of white supremacy that mean physical and spiritual violence for ourselves and our neighbors.

# Straight, Black, and Male

## What I Want White People to Know

WILLIAM J. BARBER II

Whenever I am pulled over by a police officer, introduced at a church conference, or welcomed into the halls of Congress, I am a Black man in America. But my father fought the authorities at the local hospital in Indiana where I was born to make sure that my birth certificate recorded the truth about my lineage. I am the descendant of people from Africa, from Europe, and from the Tuscaroran people who inhabited present-day North Carolina long before any European or African set foot here. While Black may be what people see when they look at me, I carry in my family history and in my DNA the complicated story of fusion that is the American story. I want white people to know that America will never be what she claims to be until we face the wounds we have inherited in this story.

To deal with the reality of racism is to face the question why this society needs me to be Black. My father was not ashamed of his Blackness or mine when he insisted that my birth certificate tell the whole truth. He understood that Black is a culture and a tradition as much as it is a "race"—that our ancestors who were told that this country did not belong to them because of the color of their skin forged a tradition of protest that has

pushed America toward a more perfect union in every generation, even as it created spaces where Black people could survive
and flourish. I am proud of that tradition and embrace it as a
gift that Black people have given this nation and the world.

But the resilience of a prisoner who survives torture does
not justify the torture—nor does it answer the question of why
a captor needs to dehumanize the person he has held against
their will. I want people who think they are white in America
to look honestly at the past and recognize that what Ta-Nehisi
Coates has said so succinctly is true: "Race is the child of racism, not the father."[1] The lies that were told to dehumanize the Indigenous people of this land and the descendants
of Africans in this place were sired to serve a purpose: they
justified the land grab and the labor arrangements that made
plantation capitalism possible. I am not Black for any other
reason than the fact that some people found Blackness to be an
effective means of building their own wealth and holding onto
power. When I note that America still needs me to be Black,
I want white people to understand how racism still props up
an unjust system.

By any measure, Black, Brown, and Native people in
America are disproportionately poorer, less healthy, and more
in danger of violence than their white neighbors. Unless you
believe that Black and Brown people are, as a group, inferior
to their white neighbors, the data make clear that racism is
systemic. To put it differently, the unequal systems that racism was born to justify continue to this day. But while those
systems disproportionately impact Black, Brown, and Native
people, they also perpetuate extreme inequality for everyone.
In raw numbers, there are more poor white people in most
US states than any other single racial group. So, if race is the
child of racism, it is also the progenitor of American inequality,
which has given rise to deaths of despair and a fake populism in
many rural parts of America.

With the Poor People's Campaign: A National Call for
Moral Revival, I've had the opportunity to travel the back-
woods of Kentucky and the hills of West Virginia in recent

years, meeting with white folks in poor counties that voted overwhelmingly for Donald Trump in 2016 and 2020. I'll never forget what one man told me about why he voted for Trump. "We knew he didn't give a damn about us," he said. "But at least he came out here. A candidate for president hadn't come out in these hills since LBJ."

What journalists call "populism" today is a mix of racism and nationalism that plays on the fear and pain of poor white people to convince them that the politicians who serve greedy corporate interests are in fact their champions. But the same people who ask poor white people for their votes use their political power to pass policies that cut taxes for corporations, deny poor people a living wage, defund public education, and slash antipoverty programs. Racism may well be the most successful con game in US history. By giving poor white people a reason to believe that they are better than their Black, Brown, and Native neighbors, greedy billionaires keep politicians in power who will not compel them to share their wealth with their fellow Americans of every race, creed, and color.

I want white Americans to know that there is a long tradition in this nation of Black, white, Brown, and Native coalitions that have joined together to challenge the systemic injustices that rich and powerful people seek to normalize. In the nineteenth century it was the abolitionist struggle, and after the Civil War it was the movement for Reconstruction. In the early twentieth century it was the labor and women's rights movements, and in the mid-twentieth century it was the Southern Freedom Struggle that we often call the "civil rights movement." In every era, the people who controlled our political and cultural institutions framed these movements as "radical" or "extreme." But they won because they were true to our deepest religious and constitutional values. And they pushed this nation toward a more perfect union.

The moral and constitutional crisis we face as a nation is, fundamentally, an identity crisis rooted in the lie of race. Shifting demographics over the past fifty years have brought us to a place where people who think they are white will soon be one among many racial minorities. If America were the land of the free and the home of the brave, truly committed to equal protection under the law, as we say we are on paper, this would not be a problem. But, as Dr. Martin Luther King once observed, "America suffers from a high blood pressure of creeds and an anemia of deeds."[2] Our stated commitment to equality has consistently been overshadowed by a majority white electorate that chooses to prop up systems that reproduce inequality. As Black, Brown, and Native people are becoming a counterbalance to that voting bloc, what is the response? The so-called populism that aims to "take back our country" by any means necessary—voter suppression, election subversion, even a riot at the US Capitol.

I want people who think they are white to recognize that they cannot have a democracy unless they are willing to face the fact that the lies they have told about me are ultimately also lies about who they are. My people taught me that no human being ever kept another human being down in a ditch without also keeping at least one foot down in that ditch themselves. The cost of plantation capitalism's inequality is an unsustainable reliance on people of every race working unsustainable hours in unjust conditions, unable to feed and shelter their families and take care of their communities. One hundred and forty million Americans are poor or low wealth today in the richest nation in the history of the world. This level of inequality is unsustainable, and the political fractures in our society are daily evidence that the bill has come due for generations of inequality.

If you need me to be Black so that you can imagine yourself to be something greater than a human being, then you have committed yourself to a lie that may well bring the whole house of this democracy down. But if in the midst of this messy story that makes us who we are you can recognize that we are, despite our faults and failures, caught up in a mutual struggle for freedom, then it is possible that we may yet reconstruct America and pass on the possibility of democracy to our children. It has been said that when a house is on fire, no one can preserve his own room. Like all of God's creatures on Noah's ark, we are in this together. We will either make it to dry land together or we will sink to the bottom of the sea on our own. But our fundamental equality is incontrovertible in the end. Whatever end we choose, we will share it together.

*Male*

# 6

## *Patriarchy's Toxic Fruit*

The single greatest moment in my baseball career came when I was ten years old (which tells you something about my athletic exploits, but we don't need to get into all that). We were playing the first-place team in our league, Hooks Alarm Company; my team, the Elks Club, was stuck somewhere in the middle of the standings. Hooks had taken a big lead with their coach's son on the mound. He was one of the harder throwers in the league and, believing the game was more or less in hand, his dad had moved him to shortstop to save some innings on the weekly innings limit—and then we'd slowly crawled back into the game. Bottom of the last inning, I was standing in the on-deck circle with the bases loaded and the score 11-8 with two outs. The Hooks coach called time-out, walked to the mound, and called his son back to the mound to pitch.

This was bad news. He'd already struck me out earlier in the game. As I stood there watching him warm up, I could hear my heart beating in my helmet. My dad, who was also my coach, broke the pounding rhythm. He got right into the earhole of my helmet and said, "No matter what happens, remember I love you, and I'm proud of you." I stepped to the plate and hit the ball over the center fielder's head for a bases-clearing triple. A few minutes later I scored the winning run. We celebrated, as ten-year-olds do, with hot dogs from the concession stand. This is a moment I have returned to over and over in my life, a touchstone of my childhood.

When I played on the high school team, we traveled a few hours away for a Saturday doubleheader against one of the tougher teams in the state. They swept both games, and I made three errors in the first inning of the first game. The ball kept finding me, but I couldn't find it. It was a long, long day. When I got home that evening, I walked past my family at the dinner table and to my room. On the door of my room were taped the pages from my dad's scorebook from that game against Hooks Alarm, with a sticky note that reminded me that I was more than my mistakes. I still have those pages.

That moment has meant different things to me at different points in my life. Then, it was about believing in myself, about the freedom that comes with realizing that the love and approval of the people who mattered to me most were not bound up in whether I got a hit or not, succeeded or failed at the things I was brave enough to try. Now, as I look back on it, I realize how unique that expression of my dad's love was. Sports dads—especially those who coach their sons—have a certain reputation. They live vicariously through their children, put pressure on them to compete and to succeed, and often model poor sportsmanship.

When I got older and became an umpire for youth baseball games, I saw things between parents and children that turned my stomach. Men who did not know how to relate to their children outside of competition, achievement, and domination pushed them beyond the point of motivation, reacting with extremes that far outweighed the cosmic importance of a summer youth baseball game, after which everyone would get popcorn and a free drink. As I have grown older, I have come to understand that my father modeled a kind of emotional vulnerability that is not all that common among men, especially in environments where winning is at stake.

My dad never knew his father, who struggled with addiction and became estranged from my grandmother early in my father's life. This is a long story that could be the subject of its own book, but we have all more or less made our peace with this aspect of our family's history. When I became a parent, it was clear to me what my dad had accomplished by being the kind of father he was, while not having his own father in his life. He had men who sacrificed for him, men who took care of him and made sure the absence of his father was not highlighted in particular situations, but by and large he was raised by his mother and grandmother. I can't help but think that this shaped the type of father he became, in a positive way—because he did not have a father around to model emotional unavailability, a father whose approval he felt he had to earn, who would teach him that vulnerability was an enemy to be avoided, a sign of weaknesses that would ultimately be preyed upon. As a result, I had a dad who wasn't afraid to tell me he loved me in the on-deck circle, *before* we won the game.

## FRAGILITY MASKED AS MASCULINITY

Too many men have come to see the withholding of any qualities associated with femininity—such as affection, sensitivity, nurture—as a strength that can give us power over others. Men are frequently in relationships with others who desire our love and approval, whether they be children or domestic partners, and yet men who had to work to receive the gift of their own father's love and approval withhold that same love and approval from their children, often as a means to motivate achievement or success. This is the opposite of the love we receive from God, who offers us love and grace without our having earned it, without the assurance that it will be returned. There is a difference between coercing and inspiring. Men who withhold expressions of their love from those who desire it can use it to dominate, whereas God's love sets free endless possibilities for

a life built on honoring and expanding that love within ourselves and in our work in the world.

This kind of love is beautiful and certainly biblical. When
Jesus was baptized, the heavens opened, the Spirit descended,
and he heard a word of affirmation from the Creator. This
was, of course, before so much—before others questioned his
authority, before folks criticized the company he kept, before
his friends let him down, before he was misunderstood, before
he was understood perfectly and labeled a threat, before he hit
his knees in Gethsemane, praying so hard his sweat fell like
drops of blood. Before all of that, he was sent into the world
with affirmation. He knew, whatever he faced, he would not
need to earn the love of the one he called Father. In the moment
of his baptism, Jesus receives the gift of being able to walk in
the world, a world in which his worthiness is constantly under
assault, without anything to prove. Whatever he would face, he
knew he was loved in a way that surpassed the outcomes of his
life. Jesus, then, has no need to dominate anyone to prove his
worth. He has no need to kill anyone to give his life meaning
or purpose. He does not need women to serve him or to prove
his virility.

I know firsthand the power of such assurance. As a son who
also received his father's affirmation, and now as a father doing
his best to give it in a lasting and meaningful way, I understand that moment to be an inoculation against the constant
barrage of challenges that may lead me to doubt my self-worth:
making the team, getting admitted to a certain college, earning a particular scholarship, pursuing a career that promises
esteem and wealth, attracting a mate. Young men are continually given ways to measure themselves other than their status
as a beloved child of God (as we all are, at various stages of life
and of varied gender identities). To a certain degree, I felt free
from these expectations.

I often how wonder how much pain the world might have
been spared if we had not concocted a version of masculinity
that wounds men, that keeps them from being the full beings
God created them to be; if men were not sent into the world

feeling as if they must be a particular kind of man to survive, which they will inevitably fail to be. Patriarchy is an expression of the deep hurt, the deep inadequacy that men feel they must live with rather than be healed from, and often that pain is expressed through violence and domination. If we cannot be fully who God made us to be, then we will make sure that no one else feels the freedom to be who God made them to be either, without incurring our wrath or ridicule. How many women have lived with daily fear of their domestic partners, how many women have had their bodies violently abused as objects for sexual gratification, how many children have been deprived of the unconditional love only a parent can give, how many young men and women have been sent off to die in wars started and maintained by men with power who were working out their individual struggle on a global stage—because men have learned to be men in ways that deprive us all of our humanity? These are the wages of patriarchy, which bell hooks helpfully defines: "Patriarchy is a political-social system that insists that males are inherently dominating, superior to everything and everyone deemed weak, especially females, and endowed with the right to dominate and rule over the weak and to maintain that dominance through various forms of psychological terrorism and violence."[1]

Given the whole of the biblical narrative, the church is uniquely gifted for subverting patriarchy and rejecting a singular definition of masculinity. The sad reality is that the church has not only reinforced but often been a major source of a masculinity built on violence, domination, and the subjugation of women. It would be difficult for patriarchy—the idea that men are ordained by God to take "leadership" over women, and women should submit to this leadership—to bear fruit of any other kind.

All kinds of elaborate theological arguments have been (and still are) made to hold two inherently contradictory statements together: women can be both valued and honored but also submissive to the leadership of men. What has traditionally been classified as "women's work"—housekeeping, caregiving, clerical work, and the like—is somehow vitally important, but beneath men. Women's contributions are significant, but women still make a fraction of what men do for the same work. As much as complementarians (those who argue that men and women serve distinctly different but complementary roles) would like to claim that women are still honored and valued in that vocation, the fruits of patriarchal culture cannot be denied. The results have meant ongoing patterns of domestic violence, the diminishment and marginalization of the gifts of women in almost every professional or academic discipline, and sexual abuse as tragic and sinful within the church as in the surrounding culture. It is difficult to imagine that patriarchy could be God's desire for humankind if God desires love and justice for the world.

Instead of offering a more just and more loving environment for women, the church has deepened the patriarchal patterns of history—not only mirrored them, but actively sustained and furthered them. Churches have been safe harbors for sexual abusers. Churches have had nothing liberative to say to women living with the daily threat of domestic partner violence. Churches have demeaned and diminished the contributions of women in our community, believing that our faith, built on the power of resurrection, can be proclaimed and explored without women at the forefront, despite women being the first to witness, believe in, and share the good news of Easter. If the church is meant to exist as an alternative to the world, then we have surely failed in this vocation when it comes to patriarchy.

We begin, once again, with confessing the truth about the ways we have constructed masculinity as a means to hold power and to deny the sacred image of God in those we identify as other.

## PATRIARCHY IS AN ABUSE OF SCRIPTURE

Men have turned to Scripture to reinforce masculine stereotypes and subjugate women in many of the same ways early white supremacists turned to the Bible to justify slavery. The places where the Bible can conceivably be interpreted to elevate the place of men and subordinate the place of women have come into sharp focus and taken on outsized importance, while the ongoing patterns in the biblical narrative that contradict the idea of patriarchy are ignored or explained away.

From the very beginning, in Genesis, our conception of the relationship between expressions of gender goes astray. The narrative allows for Eve to become the scapegoat for the fall of humanity, and women can be seen as derivative of man (formed from Adam's rib). As is the case with most Scripture, however, we tend to see what we wish to see in it. In that reading, Eve's choice is highlighted while Adam's agency is ignored. Likewise, we miss nuance in the Hebrew. *Ezer kenegdo*, which is frequently translated as "a helper suitable for him" in modern translations of Genesis 2:18, to imply that women were created to be subordinate helpers of men, is more accurately translated in a way popularized by Rachel Held Evans, as "man's perfect match . . . the help that opposes, two parts of equal weight leaning against one another."[2]

Likewise, almost everyone who has considered men, women, and issues of power in the Bible is familiar with Paul's references in Ephesians 5:22–24, 1 Corinthians 14:34–35, and 1 Timothy 2:11–12, containing instructions for the place of women both in the church and in marriage. It's telling that many disciples of Jesus know well the phrases "women keep silent" and "wives, submit to your husbands," but far fewer are familiar with the essential role so many women played in the unfolding of the story we hold sacred. In Christian tradition and in present-day Christian communities, these words from Paul have become prescriptive for women, despite their context—Paul's clear expectation that Jesus' return was imminent shaped the way he saw the world and what he believed discipleship required. This also ignores the prominent roles women apparently had in the communities to which Paul was writing. In Romans, Paul addresses Priscilla and Aquila as "coworkers in Christ" (Rom. 16:3, CEB). Phoebe is also clearly an important person in Paul's ministry; in Romans

16:1 he refers to her in Greek as *diakonos,* from which we get our term "deacon." It is difficult to imagine that these women could fulfill their roles within those communities without the opportunity to address gathered believers, or if their primary identity was related to their marital status.

Even if we acknowledge that Paul's comments and instructions on the place of women can be viewed through a patriarchal lens, there is no denying the importance of women in the whole of the biblical narrative. We see Jesus challenge social norms when he addresses the Samaritan woman, and when he calls the angry crowd on their hypocrisy when they intend to stone a woman caught in adultery. And it was the Syrophoenician woman who spoke up and challenged Jesus; she advocated for herself and called on Jesus to use his privilege for her own liberation (Mark 7:24–30).

It was a woman who became the first witness to the resurrection, and she was the first to proclaim that good news to the disciples. Of course it was. In John's Gospel, two disciples go into the tomb, and then go away. Mary Magdalene lingers and is met by a messenger, who questions her, ministers to her longing for Jesus, and opens her so that she sees that the messenger is Jesus himself (John 20:14–18). Then, she becomes a messenger herself, uniquely equipped to tell the story of Jesus' power to bring life out of death, because she has known it for her own heart and soul. In Luke, the angels come to her (as well as Joanna, Mary the mother of James, and some other women who come to attend to the body of Jesus while the men who followed him are huddled in fear)—not to the Beloved Disciple, not to Peter, the foundation on which the church would eventually be built. They appear to her, it seems to me, because who else was equipped to hear a word of resurrection, to know and see and go and tell the good news of resurrection, except one who had been dead and had been brought to life herself? Who else has the imagination necessary to believe that blood and sweat and pain and grief could and would accompany the arrival of new life in the world? The men who heard it first dismissed it as an idle tale.

It should be no surprise, then, that Mary Magdalene's place among the early followers of Jesus was actively diminished in the early years of the church; by the fourth century, Mary was (intentionally) conflated with other Marys in the Gospel narrative, and the common association that emerged was that Mary Magdalene had been a prostitute.[3] Of course, this undermined Mary's place in the narrative as a faithful disciple, leader, and proclaimer of the gospel, and Pope Gregory the Great used this narrative to justify keeping women out of the priesthood.[4] As a result, in the twenty first century, my clergy colleagues who are women are asked to connect people to the minister when they answer the phone in their church offices and are frequently passed over by ecclesial decision makers when it comes to leadership in churches, especially prominent ones. Not least of all, we lose a vivid characterization and a story worth exploration in Mary Magdalene. When we miss or minimize these women, we miss some of the most beautiful elements of the biblical narrative.

There are other stories involving women in the Bible that amplify themes of love and justice that many of us have missed; these stories take themes easily generalized and make them specific—they color in the lines in beautiful ways. Take, for example, the daughters of Zelophehad: Mahlah, Noah, Hoglah, Milcah, and Tirzah in Numbers 27. They are women in a patriarchal culture who demand what is theirs. Property was passed from males to males, meaning that after the death of their father in the wilderness, they would receive nothing. These five sisters seek their rightful inheritance from Moses, who was once in their shoes himself, petitioning the powerful Pharaoh to let the enslaved Hebrews go. And in this moment, the tables are turned. Moses holds the power within the community; he is the chief human lawmaker among the body, and the people trust that what he tells them is from the mouth of God. Even from within a liberated people comes a call from these Brown women for further and deeper liberation. Their courage to speak changes the law.

Consider Shiphrah and Puah. There would be no Moses without Shiphrah and Puah, the Hebrew midwives who, you

could say, began the movement of liberation for the Israelites with one of the earliest acts of civil disobedience. At the
beginning of the book of Exodus, the king commands the
Hebrew midwives to kill any boys they deliver. The king
is using death to preserve power, afraid that if the Israelites
become too numerous, they will no longer tolerate their subjugation and enslavement. But the midwives will not have
it. They resist, and persist in bringing life into the world,
and they do it by using the king's own prejudice against
him, playing into the subhuman stereotypes he has about the
Hebrew people—that they are not as fair and sensitive as the
Egyptian women. In the end, a racial stereotype that brings
about a violent policy becomes a tool for undercutting that
same policy. The Bible is wonderful this way. What a shame
it is to miss these vital stories, especially because we are wor-
ried about the implications of elevating the place of women
in our cultural and religious life.

Too often, we have seen in the Bible what we wish to see;
rather than persistent questions that undermine our understandings of power and relationship, we have seen our own
prejudices and insecurities affirmed, even justified. If you come
to the Bible with a desire to seize power over women—sexual,
political, economic, or physical power—there is enough to
twist to fit your agenda, but it requires a flat, unimaginative,
ahistorical reading of the Bible to get there. Unfortunately,
men have too often found it easier to live with that than with
the notion that we are called to do and be more than what we
have learned from the patterns of behavior we have inherited.


## PATRIARCHY IS ABOUT DENIAL

Masculinity is often defined by what it withholds, most obvi-
ously emotion. Among men, it is a virtue to be "tough," meaning that we refuse any kind of emotion that might make us
feel (or appear) vulnerable. Vulnerability implies weakness,
and among men who see themselves in a kind of animalistic

competition to dominate their competition and find a mate, there is no place for weakness. How many of us had fathers who scarcely ever cried? How many who rarely allowed themselves outward expressions of love or grief? How many men had fathers who, when we were hurting, told us to "suck it up" or "be tough" or even "be a man"? This is why the story I told at the beginning of this chapter has had such lasting meaning for me—in that situation, my dad broke the paradigm and was vulnerable with me, in a moment when he knew I also felt vulnerable, *in the midst of a competition* where other men and their sons were competing at what seemed like much more than baseball. My dad has been expressive in this way more times than I can remember. He has (seemingly) never been afraid to express sadness or joy or grief, to grab and hold me close in moments when he is intensely proud or knows I am hurting. It is noteworthy because it seems he is the exception among men of his generation, not the rule.

To be truthful, however, men desire love and approval in the ways all humans do. We hurt when that love is lost or missing, we doubt ourselves when we are rejected, we feel the pain of the deep wounds that often accompany being human, but there is too much currency in our withholding these emotions from those around us for us to express them. First, to break with common masculine stereotypes is to risk the rejection of one's peers. Patriarchy socializes boys to rid themselves of "feminine" characteristics, because the feminine is identified as inferior, and because to demonstrate "feminine" characteristics when those characteristics do not match one's genitalia deviates from prescribed norms and is threatening.

Both homophobia and transphobia have their roots in patriarchy; when men conceive of women as weaker and subservient, and when we derive our own identity from the power we are able to have over women, men who do not conform to those ideals and women free from any need of men pose a particular threat. These are the complex dynamics at work in something as (unfortunately) commonplace as bullying. In his book *The Man They Wanted Me to Be*, Jared Yates Sexton describes his own experience of socialization that seemed intent on weeding out "feminine" qualities like "sensitivity, curiosity, creativity, weakness and a desire to communicate past the purposes of utility." He found acceptance when he learned the accepted rhythms of speech, of interaction, and sufficient skill at sports. The patriarchal system that reinforces this version of masculinity and femininity "works on the basis of positive and negative reinforcement. Behave as a traditional male and receive entry into the group. Fail and receive physical, emotional, and social abuse until you have no choice but to conform."[5]

Because men are human beings who long for the acceptance of others they identify as peers, this conditioning is effective. Over time, men learn to deny feelings, interests, or manners of expression within themselves as the sacrifice necessary for belonging in the culture in which they live. We would sooner conform than risk isolation. Ironically, isolation comes for us anyway. We wall ourselves off from particular emotions, which means it is impossible to understand fully what brings us joy, what matters most, what offers us fulfillment. Not only that, it creates barriers in our relationships with others, when those who seek our love, who we want to love well, suffer from our inability to be fully who we are. When we conform, we sacrifice the full expression of our humanity, the freedom to discover who God is calling us to be, and the self-exploration that makes human life meaningful. Who I might be in light of Jesus' call on my life is limited—if not eliminated—by confining that person to the limits of performative masculinity.

Early on, we learn to deny a self we may never come to know. The author bell hooks points out that "anyone who has a false self must be dishonest. People who learn to lie to themselves and others cannot love because they are crippled in their capacity to tell the truth and therefore unable to trust."[6] The force of patriarchy, pressing down on men to conform to a certain version of masculinity, alienates men from themselves and one another. If I cannot be honest with myself, then I cannot be honest with you; and if I cannot be honest with you, then our relationships exist only on these pretenses, and they lack authenticity. Human beings were made for community—to be in relationship with God and each other, to enter into the kind of intimacy we are taught to fear. Jesus frequently draws these secrets out of those he encounters—the vulnerability within themselves that they have spent their lives carefully obscuring. Consider Zacchaeus, trying to observe Jesus from a safe distance, only to have Jesus call out his veiled curiosity and draw out his desire for something different from a life built on exploitation. He only wanted to get a glimpse! Jesus calls those who would follow him to engaged, examined lives, animated by love and compassion.

Moreover, it seems Jesus possessed a kind of affection for those around him that he did not attempt to hide from them or others. When his friend Lazarus died, Jesus wept openly. When looking out over Jerusalem, he expressed pain at their rejection of his love (Matt. 23:37). When he saw someone in pain, he was moved with compassion; translated literally, his stomach churned. He acknowledged his need for rest and took it. When he hung on the cross, he expressed his pain and grief. Simply put, Jesus does not conform to our conceptions of masculinity, despite the efforts of patriarchal thinkers who wish to place Jesus among traditional understandings of masculinity. We who would follow him, then, are not called to bring to bear only the veiled versions of ourselves that fit within the frameworks we have constructed together; we have but one life, here, and patriarchy demands we cut ourselves off from so much of what it has to give.

## PATRIARCHY HARMS OUR RELATIONSHIPS WITH WOMEN

If it alienates us from ourselves and from other men, then consider what implications patriarchy has for our relationships with women. If it is undesirable to display characteristics associated with femininity, we reach the logical conclusions that result in misogyny—the internalized prejudice against women associated with patriarchy. This prejudice shows up everywhere, from the malpractice in biblical interpretation I outlined above, to unequal pay for equal work, to rape culture that sees women as outlets for the supposedly uncontrollable sexual urges of men. Men, socialized to cut themselves off from much of what it is to be human, learn to derive primary aspects of their identity from their ability to feel superior to women (if this sounds similar to patterns of whiteness, and the need for whiteness to alleviate underlying insecurity, it is); if I must shape who I am to conform to patriarchal values, then I will also deny the women around me the opportunity to be free in the way God has granted. The privilege we believe it creates is more accurately called alienation. What kind of relationships are possible between men and women when women must always be cognizant of the risk of physical violence and sexual abuse? When there is a subtext of fear and vulnerability just beneath the surface—even in our closest relationships—how much can we know of and be known by another?

What does it do to us to be perpetually feared? While attending the Poor People's Campaign Moral Congress in the spring of 2019 in Washington, DC, I stayed with a friend in the Maryland suburbs. I drove from his home to the commuter rail station each morning to take the train into the city. I returned late in the evening, walking along the platform and across the parking lot in spotty lighting. It seemed like each night there was a woman, alone, in front of me. I wondered what was the best way to manage myself, knowing that she was clocking my presence, and wondered what narrative was in her mind. How did she perceive my footsteps? How did it make her feel that I was behind her, making her that much more vulnerable? What mental preparation was she making, in the event that this was the moment she feared? I thought it best to quicken my pace and get in front of her; then at least she could have eyes on me, but then I wondered how she might perceive my quickened pace, approaching her from behind. In the end, I chose to pass her, but with wide berth to give her some space. Whether this was the best choice, I couldn't say.

This is a small, anecdotal story. But these moments occur every day—in elevators, stairwells, parking lots, boardrooms . . . and in bedrooms and kitchens as well. While these are voluntary considerations for men, the women in our lives are forced to think about these things all the time—carrying car keys between their fingers in dark parking lots, consuming only drinks they saw prepared, positioning themselves to avoid the man who doesn't respect personal boundaries. When fear persists between us, as bell hooks points out, it keeps us away from love. Or, as we read in 1 John 4:18, "There is no fear in love, but perfect love casts out fear; for fear has to do with punishment." Many of us would believe there is strength in being feared, believing that this fear is a sign of respect of, or deference to, power. This is a lie, and a seductive one. Instead, this fear is a rift in our relationships to our neighbors; and if we stand alienated from our neighbors, then we are also alienated from God.

Patriarchy requires denial. It demands that men deny themselves—their emotions, fears, and vulnerabilities—in the interest of conforming to patriarchal norms. It also demands that we deny the sacred image of God in women, undervaluing their gifts and abilities and regarding their bodies only as objects that bear the brunt of physical aggression, vehicles for sexual expression and childbearing. During the campaign for the 2016 presidential election, the infamous *Access Hollywood* tape leaked to the media, in which Donald Trump could be heard making crude references to a woman's anatomy and expressing his preference to initiate sexual contact without consent. This was ultimately dismissed as "locker room talk" by the eventual president and scores of other apologists—women among them. In one sense, the president was right. I have heard graphic descriptions of female anatomy and crude references to sex in locker rooms, though all the ones I can recall took place among teenage boys (not that they are excused). There *are* grown men who talk like this among one another; where these apologists were very, very wrong was in reacting as if this kind of language is no big deal. One in five women in America report being the victim of an attempted or completed rape in their lifetimes, and a whopping 83 percent of women report being the victim of sexual harassment or assault (emphasis on *report*—how many were never reported or weren't taken seriously?).[7]

Given the focus on the creation story in Genesis by so many arguing for biblical patriarchy, it is ironic that humankind being created in the image of God has been so underplayed. Our bodies do amazing things for us and enable us to do meaningful things for one another. Moreover, Jesus had a body and lived among us. This being the case, we cannot disdain bodies as objects simply for use and abuse, whether our own or another's. I talk to my sons a lot about having respect for their bodies. What I try to teach them is to treat their bodies as the holy vessels they are—that when they disrespect their own bodies, they dishonor God's creation. We don't toss trash out of the window, we recycle our glass and our plastic, and we honor the bodies God has given us as best we can—all are acts of worship that remember the imprint of God on every aspect of God's creation. My hope is that, having learned to respect their own bodies, they will not grow to view the bodies of others as objects for their own use, and they will draw healthy boundaries around how they give their bodies to others.

Patriarchy, in its view of women as complementary to men, invites men to believe and act as if the bodies of women also exist for the fulfillment of men. Entire industries exist for the purpose of making women's bodies more desirable for men, and the boundaries we give to our young women, especially, teach them that they are responsible for how men perceive their bodies. School dress codes go to much greater lengths to dictate the clothing of young women, since the amount of flesh exposed may serve as a distraction (or, to use Christian patriarchal language, a "stumbling block") to those who may find them attractive. The laws and health care policies that dictate the kind of medical coverage and care that women receive are written and enforced primarily by men. In her book *Resist and Persist*, Erin Wathen writes about the rape trial in Steubenville, Ohio, that involved a number of football players from the high school. Under oath, one of the players testified that they viewed the victim as "community property.[8]

Community property. That is exactly what Donald Trump expressed on that bus, when he presumed he could grab women by their genitals—that the body of whatever woman he chose must exist to fulfill his own desires, as if it could belong to him, or anyone. When this tape leaked, I assumed immediately—as did so many others—that this was the end of his presidential candidacy, especially since so many Christians had supported him, believing that he would protect and further Christian values in America. Surely, such a crass, dehumanizing diatribe that contradicts everything God desires for us would be enough for people of faith to demand better. I should have known this would not be the case.

Despite our well-developed theology relating to what humans should do with their bodies, patriarchy still allows for the sacred image of God in women to be diminished by men who view the bodies of women as created by God, but for their use. As Wathen says, "Control is the patriarchy's bottom line: control our bodies; control the space in which we can live, work and just be; control the roles we can assume, the voices we are allowed, the face we can make in public. It's all about control. We are even led to want to control and contain our own figures—Spanx, underwires, control-top pantyhose. It is all about holding in and manipulating what nature gave us for our own."[9]

On the other side of the coin was Trump's running mate, Mike Pence, who made headlines when he explained his use of the "Graham rule," referencing the Rev. Billy Graham's practice of never being alone with a woman other than his wife; this presumes, of course, that every interaction between men and women has the undercurrent of sex, and that either the men cannot trust themselves or the women they encounter might exercise their sexuality as power over them. The rise of the #MeToo movement has indeed brought increased scrutiny to interactions between men and women, particularly when issues of power and authority are at play in the workplace and elsewhere. For every man who has complained in public about the anxiety this supposed risk of false accusation has brought to his life and his interactions with women, there are multiples who have said so to one another behind closed doors. This discomfort is a tell. It demonstrates an awareness of women's bodies and boundaries that did not exist before, and it is an acknowledgment that men have not generally considered how their physical presence impacted the women around them before. There is great irony in men now fearing the repercussions of physical contact with women, when this has always been a necessary state of mind for women.

In order for women's bodies to be respected in the way their identities in the sight of God require, we will need more than the passage of time, more than an increase in the presence of women in leadership. Indeed, this has not made things better, but could make things worse. Wathen argues: "As women gain traction in leadership, rights, and public autonomy, it's no wonder that sexual assault statistics pretty much stay at alarmingly high rates. When women find voice in public life, the patriarchy finds ways to silence and subdue them."[10]

The harm patriarchal culture has done to women is immeasurable. For centuries, men have used women as the outlet for our own brokenness—our insecurities, our inability to feel and express emotion, the anger and frustration we feel because we do not understand ourselves and are working constantly to conform to a version of manhood that asks us to be something we are not. In making "weakness" our enemy, we have also made the vulnerability we fear into a weapon we can use against the very people we often claim to love the most. To feel powerful, we work to assert our physical dominance over those whose bodies we feel we can possess, for pleasure or for harm. To feel strong, we avoid that which might test our strength, instead forging barriers between ourselves and those whose love we both need and desire but fear losing. To feel successful, we minimize the competition, pushing the gifts and talents of women to the margins so that they do not threaten our sense of competence. To feel whole, we project our brokenness onto those around us.

In addition to the harm patriarchy has done to women—that we can account for, and that we cannot—it has cost us untold moments of truth and beauty in our own lives. That moment of tenderness between my dad and me has held currency for us, and it is a moment we have returned to over and over again in our lives. One moment of vulnerability, one moment of expression, one moment of truth shared, shaped me in ways so profound that I sit, now, recounting it for you, as I have in sermons and in conversations and in talks with men's ministries previously. It is so small and yet, I believe, a testament to how precariously the masculinity we have inherited exists. As the father of boys, I see how my choices about the man I am impact them.

One son riffles through papers at the end-of-year parent-teacher conference, afraid that if I take too long to linger on any of them, I may find fault and not approval. I watch one's face when I raise my voice in anger or frustration, the sadness and defeat that he feels in an instant when he believes he has disappointed me. These remind me of the power I am given—to make them whole, or to shatter them into pieces. These are daily choices, daily opportunities that place me again in the on-deck circle . . . only this time I am on the other side, able to whisper over the thumping heartbeats of vulnerable ones trying to find their place in the world, wondering if who they are is enough in the sight of God. It is. And I want them to know it, so that they do not go looking for that knowledge in all the wrong places.

# 7

## *Detoxifying Masculinity*

It is not lost on me that what it took for me to have an expressive, healthy relationship with my dad was for him to be deprived of the experience of being raised by his own father. It is certainly possible that he might've become the person he is, and raised me as he and my mother did, without the experience of being raised by women, but it is difficult to imagine.

Despite the ways that the cycle of toxic masculinity was broken for me, patriarchy—like racism—is not only individual but systemic. It is a way of distributing power, or withholding it, and it is possible for the patriarchal structure of our culture to persist without chauvinists. This means that having a father who did not feel the need to match all the macho stereotypes that the culture perpetuates did not spare me the formation of a patriarchal mind-set that must be deconstructed, and reconstructed, over and over again. My wife still has to seek out vulnerability from me. I still find myself wanting my kids to share my love of sports, even though sports, when it comes down to it, are of no cosmic importance and have little to do with the kind of people they will become. Sorting through a stack of résumés for potential administrative assistants, I find myself being dismissive of the candidates who are men, because this work has so traditionally been associated with women. These are only the things I'm mindful of, and they do nothing to address patriarchy as a way of distributing power or withholding it; it is possible for the patriarchal structure of our culture to persist without chauvinists, and my little self-corrections will not do much to topple it either. It is not enough to be sensitive, or mindful, or a defender of women. There are whole systems created to sustain and perpetuate patriarchal culture. To that end, in reconstructing ourselves and our world without patriarchal values, perhaps we can begin inward, and move outward.

## LIVE AN EXAMINED LIFE

I remember my earliest experiences with men's ministry gatherings. The men's ministry in my hometown would gather for breakfast on a Saturday morning at a diner. There was small talk, coffee, grits, and bacon. Then the group would drive down the road to the woodlot run by the Salvation Army. At the woodlot, we would split and stack firewood for those in the community who heated their homes with wood-burning stoves, then load the wood into the beds of pickup trucks and deliver it in the community. It was the prototypical church activity for men—there was food, manual labor, and the opportunity to serve our neighbors, and we didn't need to have one meaningful conversation for it to happen.

As a pastor, I've come to believe that this kind of time spent together in Christian community is important; it is an opportunity for us to know one another and develop relationships that can be called upon when and if significant events take place in our lives, when those relationships are particularly useful. It lays the groundwork for the kind of communities we see formed by early Christians in Acts, where there was devotion to a shared material and spiritual life.

But those relationships are only useful for men if we are willing to live examined lives, to know ourselves in such a way that we can offer ourselves to one another. In Luke, when Jesus tells the parable of the Prodigal Son, the critical moment that changes the trajectory of the son's life happens when he has reached rock bottom. He has squandered his inheritance in "dissolute living" and has a job among pigs, representing how far he has strayed from the values of the family that raised him. In that moment, Jesus says, he "'came to himself'" (Luke 15:17). This phrase holds so much. Perhaps, in this moment, the prodigal was finally able to see himself as he was, to see the patterns of use and abuse that had led to fractured relationships with his family and his own suffering. This kind of reckoning is painful; one might see what one has been blind to, a version of one's self that brings shame and embarrassment.

If we stay in the shallows, if we do not risk thinking too deeply about our own existence, and about how that existence impacts those around us, we are spared coming face-to-face with our failures, spared the kind of the relationships it would be painful to lose, spared the hard work of being accountable for the person we offer to those around us. Manhood, for all its talk about toughness, rewards an inward life devoid of experiences that could bring pain or challenge. So much of what Jesus does for those who would follow him is to bring them face-to-face with themselves, as they are—think of Peter in the courtyard of the high priest, hearing the cock crow in the distance; think of Zacchaeus, held accountable for stealing from his neighbors; or the angry mob, prepared to stone to death the woman accused of adultery, asked to take account of their own sinfulness ("Let him who is without sin cast the first stone").

Somehow, we have created Christian communities where it is entirely possible to actively participate without ever having to look inward, to do the hard work of confronting those places within ourselves that are necessary for transformation. All those men, sipping coffee and catching up on what's happening in each other's work lives or home lives, could go about serving their neighbors on a Saturday morning, with perfectly good intentions, but still go home and never have a deep conversation with their wives or their kids. And if we are not awake and alive to ourselves, and to one another, then we cannot become fully who God created us to be.

One of the television shows I watched and often found hilarious was the sitcom *Everyone Loves Raymond*. I watched it in syndication, mostly, and initially found it a hilarious depiction of suburban life. The longer I watched, however, the more I came to resent the way Raymond, the protagonist, was depicted. He was aloof and awkward, emotionally shallow and always struggling to relate to his parents, his wife, his brother, and his children. His situation as a sex-starved, romantically inept partner was a trope the writers returned to over and over again. Every week, Raymond's lack of self-awareness caused him to run afoul of his wife, and he would need to redeem himself by the end of the half hour. His father was even worse: a brash, rude, insensitive curmudgeon, he could summon some tenderness with enough cajoling and sufficient humor to cover the moment. Ultimately, Raymond's desire for intimacy with his wife was painted as a purely animalistic male instinct, not at all related to his adolescent emotional maturity. It was funny because it carried a hint of truth, because those who watched on weeknights saw themselves or their husbands or their fathers in Raymond and his family; but therein lies the sad reality of masculinity, where being emotionally immature or unavailable is simply part of the equation—an obstacle to overcome, but one that ultimately sees no change or evolution.

The "sex-starved" husband we so often see in our stereotypes of marriage is too shallow—as if men are only capable of acting on animal instinct and are uncomplicated emotional beings who only need physical intimacy in a relationship. The standard this stereotype sets for young men is harmful in that it encourages them to cut themselves off from the strength of their feelings and the vulnerability that comes with them. Unfortunately, the results are shallow relationships and satisfying needs that have an emotional element in only physical ways. To have full relationships, we must be connected to the fullness of our feelings, to our own needs—where they come from and how they are met.

We could begin, then, by making our men's ministries more than coffee and manual labor, but instead projects in cultivating emotional awareness and spiritual growth. If we can create Christian communities where men can be vulnerable and realize that there is life on the other side of that vulnerability, it is possible that our churches will not be so conducive to men who seek their own fulfillment through the use and abuse of the women in their midst. This begins with pastors and other leaders who are willing to model this kind of vulnerability, who can be open about the cultivation of their own inner lives, particularly and especially the ways they are learning to leave behind versions of masculinity that have not served their discipleship.

## MAKE ROOM

In many Protestant churches of the sixteenth to nineteenth centuries, a token was required for admittance to the Lord's Table for Communion. The clergy would visit members of the community to determine if they had made adequate preparations for receiving the sacrament, and if so, give them a token that provided admittance.

In my tradition, the celebration of Communion at the Lord's Table is of utmost importance. We gather at the Table every week, and it is the element of worship to which all others point. Alexander Campbell, foundational thinker of the Stone-Campbell movement, had an experience that sparked this theology. In his Presbyterian church in early-nineteenth-century Glasgow, Campbell had received a Communion token. When the plate came around for the collection of these tokens, Campbell angrily tossed his in the plate, and then when the bread and wine followed, he refused to partake and stormed out in protest. This was essentially the end of his place in the Presbyterian Church, and a move toward the formation of what he called a restorationist movement, which has become the Christian Church (Disciples of Christ).

I understand his protest. What does it mean for us to be gatekeepers, keeping out those who seek to know and experience the mystery of Communion for themselves? The system was ripe for the abuse and misuse of this power—for some to restrict the access of others based on criteria that may or may not have anything to do with what it means to receive the Lord's Supper faithfully.

Within the church and the wider culture, we still restrict access to power and leadership as if there is limited space, as if more for some will mean less for others. The legacy of patriarchy means that men can often be gatekeepers for women trying to make their way in fields dominated by men. Ultimately, the choice is whether or not to behave as if we fear relinquishing the power we may have over women in these systems. If we fear a meritocracy, if we fear giving way to women who may be more qualified, the strength we convey as men is more fiction than truth. Perhaps we are not secure enough in our own gifts to believe that if the gifts and talents of women are increasingly visible and recognized (the gifts and talents of women have always been indispensable, whether or not those women have received credit), the role and gifts of men will somehow be diminished. Some of the most dynamic pastors and best preachers I know are women, and as a result the churches they lead are more adaptive to the changing realities of the church in America. The choice I have is to be threatened by their gifts or to celebrate them. To be threatened by them would be a detriment to the institution I serve; the more churches flourish, the greater the possibilities for my own ministry. What advances might be made in STEM fields or in business or—God help us—government if gender were not a primary qualification, if the men who held power in those fields were willing to nurture and embrace the gifts and talents of women where they have historically been diminished.

Some churches, moved by the best of intentions to place a woman in leadership, will do so without addressing the latent patriarchal tendencies present in the congregation. This means that they are inviting women into leadership where they will inevitably suffer the consequences of the ensuing power struggle. My colleagues in ministry who are women deal with these consequences all the time: sexually suggestive comments and inappropriate physical contact from male parishioners, poor policies on maternity leave, challenges to their leadership from men who are resistant to being led by a woman. It doesn't need to be a majority of the church in order for these things to be harmful and to create an environment where women feel threatened—and no one can flourish in an environment where they must always be defending themselves and mindful of justifying their place.

Erin Wathen offers helpful practical steps toward accepting women as leaders, including inviting guest preachers who are women if the staff is primarily made up of men, or inviting girls from the youth group to take a prominent role on Sunday mornings, or building interfaith relationships with neighboring faith communities where women play prominent roles.[1] In the church I serve, both pastors are straight white men, which means, on the vast majority of Sundays, the congregation hears preaching from a particular worldview. No matter how much I learn about patriarchy, about issues of faith and gender, I still see the world (and the gospel) through that lens. The church needs to hear from women; our people, young and old, need to see women in the pulpit, behind the Lord's Table, interceding on behalf of God's people in prayer.

It is not enough to be passive in this struggle to have women's voices prioritized in Christian communities. Progress, to repeat Martin Luther King's phrase, does not "roll in on wheels of inevitability." It is possible for the church to claim its vocation as a change agent of the culture rather than simply measuring and reflecting the temperature of the surrounding culture (at best), but we cannot do that without being proactive in seeking out the voices of women.

These seem like healthy places to begin, if this is a growing edge for a Christian community. Even in "progressive" communities that brand themselves as justice-minded, bent on undoing patriarchal white supremacy, misogynistic tendencies are still present; they're baked into the culture. Awareness and course correction are always necessary, and this cannot be done without amplifying the voices of the women in our midst and giving them credit for their contributions.

Too often throughout history, women's insights and influence have been ignored, downplayed, and left out of the curriculum. One example is the life and work of Frances Perkins, the first woman to serve as a member of a presidential cabinet. Perkins was a witness to the horrific fire at the Triangle Shirtwaist factory, and the experience compelled her to a life in community organizing around labor rights and workplace safety. She rose in prominence as a community leader and was eventually selected by President Franklin Delano Roosevelt to be his labor secretary. Her work at this critical juncture in American history is still part of our lives. Many of us learned that FDR launched America's "social safety net" programs: Social Security, unemployment insurance, the forty-hour workweek, and the minimum wage, not to mention regulations on safe working conditions and child labor laws. In reality, the creator and advocate for these changes was Frances Perkins. Behind the scenes, she was also the architect of many aspects of FDR's New Deal, which helped lift America out of the Great Depression. Her impact was not limited to economic issues. During the rise of Hitler in Germany, many European Jews sought sanctuary in the United States and were denied. As labor secretary, Frances Perkins was also responsible for the Immigration and Naturalization Service. She circumvented the people in power who were reluctant to accept those seeking asylum by using her position to increase the number of visitor visas granted to European Jews fleeing the Nazis—then never enforced the expiration dates on those visas.

This was a history I did not know. I took history courses in high school and college without ever learning her name. Frances Perkins's life was not easy—she faced all kinds of personal and professional hardships, not least of which was that when things were going poorly, she often took the blame, and when her ideas succeeded, the credit often went to someone else. In reality, she changed the course of American history as much as any other twentieth-century politician. No doubt, this is a pattern many women know; many of their contributions, however significant, are buried "behind the scenes" by white men who wish to receive the credit. One way we learn to amplify the voices of women in our present moment is to tell the truth about the women in our past who have made us who we are but never got the recognition they deserved.

Nothing about the success of a woman is threatening, as long as I derive my value from God who has claimed me and loves me, and not from the standards of patriarchy. Ultimately, removing the boundaries we have created around the place of women in leadership of all kinds serves all of us in ways that amplify everyone's gifts and abilities. Men would be well served to accept that there are women whose gifts surpass their own in certain areas. We serve one another and the world best when we understand our limitations and do not assume that because we are men we must be gifted in particular areas. Paul's familiar image of the human body and its various parts in 1 Corinthians 12 reminds us that the body is in need of many gifts; assigning gender restraints to various gifts has surely put many men in places where they are not equipped to be (and worse, given the many instances where men, under the influence of toxic masculinity, have committed grave sins while in leadership), and vice versa. There is room for everyone, and we all stand to gain when more seats are filled.

## REJECT GENDERED STEREOTYPES

Two contradictory things happened when my wife and I had boys. One, I immediately began to imagine us having so many of the quintessential father-and-son moments I had with my own dad. I could see us playing catch in the backyard; sitting in the driveway listening to UNC basketball on the car radio because games were too intense for us to risk missing something in the thirty seconds it would take to move inside and watch on the living room TV. When my oldest son was young, I started his first baseball card collection before he could recognize a single team or player. I pictured myself serving as best man at their weddings (to women), and when my youngest son finally took an interest in Carolina basketball and asked to watch the replay of a basketball game that ended past his bedtime, I thought I might cry real tears of joy and pride.

At the same time, however, I was acutely aware that I did not want to force gender stereotypes on them. I tried to prepare myself mentally for the idea that they might not be into trucks or *Star Wars* or sports at all, tried not to sort things into "boy" toys and "girl" toys, tried to resist suggesting that certain colors are more feminine than others (though for a long time I would not have been caught dead in a pink shirt myself). I suppose what I wanted was to see movement away from gendered stereotypes, but I did not want my own family to be on the leading edge of that movement. I cannot say that it was because I was afraid of the social consequences for them, or for me, or that I was afraid it would make some kind of statement about me or them. I think it was simply a failure of imagination. Could I imagine for myself, and for them, a life other than the one prescribed by the norms so ingrained in me? Could I imagine them not bringing home girlfriends? Not high-fiving them in the stands after a touchdown, as I'd done with my own dad?

I did not—do not—know how I would feel if reality fell far outside the bounds of those expectations, and we often fear what we do not know. I hope I would take an interest in whatever they are interested in, and be happy and content when they are happy and content. I would like to think that I am developing the emotional maturity it takes to recognize that who I am is not lessened if my children do not follow in my footsteps. Our children need parents who do not inject their own maturation into their struggles to grow up.

Even though I was mindful of gendered stereotypes and why they are problematic, my boys still picked up on them. They still identified pink as a "girl color" and still categorize certain things as being for girls only. This is because gender stereotypes are pervasive in our culture. Walk down the toy aisles in your local superstore. One is almost uniformly pink and purple, filled with dolls and toys for pretend cooking or caregiving. Another is filled with trucks and guns and balls and "action figures," mostly in primary colors. Perhaps children do gravitate to one or the other naturally—I swear our boys had an innate ability to mimic the sounds of motors—but this happens so early in a child's development, it is difficult to know. One problem with these stereotypes is that they teach children that if they do not naturally conform to these identities, there is something wrong with them, or they have failed in some way to be what is expected of them.

The other problem with stereotyped gender norms is that, for men particularly, they often reinforce attributes that run counter to the way of discipleship. Principal among these is violence. Boys learn early on that they should be willing to fight and that they should find a certain kind of violence entertaining. This creates a significant dissonance with Jesus, who refused to defend himself when the officers of the court came to arrest him, who rebuked Peter for his use of violence in defense of his life. It makes it difficult to be reconciled to the Jesus we find in the Sermon on the Mount, who teaches us to turn the other cheek and go the extra mile, to be more creative in our resistance to those who would do us harm than returning violence for violence. How is it that we put together a Jesus who rides in triumphantly on a donkey (of all things) and bows down to serve his disciples on their last night together with the notion that the role of a man is to dominate, to conquer, to be served? It is a recipe for constructing our understanding of Jesus around our conceptions of masculinity, to read the values we find on the toy aisle into the Bible because, of the two, the Bible is easier to ignore than the demands of the culture in which we live.

Before our children have the opportunity to form any way of understanding themselves and to discern what the way of Jesus may ask of them, they are shaped by gender stereotypes that will make self-determination difficult. We should be honest that Christians are not in the business of raising children to be whatever they want to be; ultimately, we are raising them to encounter God, to know the story of liberation we find in the Bible, to be shaped by the person and work of Jesus. Within the journey, there is room for self-determination that is deep and wide. Our children can be free to discern who they are without masculinity and femininity being defined in ways that limit their exploration and invite shame into their lives as a coercive force. The imaginations of children are much more vivid than those of the adults charged with raising them. The path to liberation for them, and for us, is to be free enough to imagine loving realities far, far outside the ones the world imagines for us.

## CHECK OTHER MEN

To return to the *Access Hollywood* tape of then reality-TV star Donald Trump, we might consider also the role of Billy Bush, the TV host heard on tape awkwardly responding to Trump's bragging. When the tape became public, Bush's role also came under scrutiny because he had failed to challenge Trump's graphic and misogynistic language. Most men reading this have witnessed language or behavior that is abusive, either directed toward a woman or, nearly as harmful, behind closed doors, though perhaps not as explicit as Trump's.

The #MeToo movement has been (in part) about women seizing power and raising their voices to reinforce lines men have been willing to cross whenever they felt like it—emotional, verbal, and physical lines that mark the boundaries of personal dignity. However, the reality of patriarchal culture is that men are more inclined to accept a challenge from other men. When attitudes that can and do manifest themselves in ways that are harmful go unchecked—a man talks about grabbing a woman by the genitals and receives only a knowing laugh—then the chances he actualizes that behavior grow. Conversely, when those we see as peers challenge the values we hold and the language and behavior we practice, perhaps there is greater opportunity for a pause, reflection, and transformation.

Fred Craddock tells a story about a late-night study session for his New Testament exam while he was in seminary. He took a break to walk to the diner for a bite to eat. While he was there, eating his meal, a Black man came into the diner to order food. Craddock watched as the cook took up the charred remains of a burger from the back corner of the griddle, placed it plain on a bun, and handed it in a napkin to the man, who sat on the sidewalk to eat. Recalling this moment, Craddock faces the reality that he neither did nor said anything about the injustice that was taking place right in front of him. And, in the kind of punch-in-the-gut ending Craddock was famous for, he remembers walking out in the street after he'd finished his meal and hearing somewhere, off in the distance, what he could swear was the sound of a cock crow.[2]

He is referencing, of course, Peter's denial of Jesus in the courtyard of the high priest. Like Peter, we too often remain silent when presented with opportunities to lay claim to our discipleship. We deny Jesus all the time. When acting in keeping with our allegiance to Jesus will mean consequences in relationships we feel are important, we tend to stay quiet even if we know immediately that our silence is complicity in something harmful. There are times when standing up to wrong is self-serving or done for the sake of appearance, like the "white knight" who defends a woman in a social situation in the interest of endearing himself to her. Indeed, there is the opportunity to slip into masculine stereotypes in these instances, which is why conversations among men are so important. All of us are steeped in and conditioned by the values of patriarchy, which means that while there may be moments when we can see clearly their effects unfolding around us, it is just as likely we will be acting them out ourselves.

To enter into Christian community is to accept the vocation of challenging and being challenged. In Matthew 18, Jesus outlines this aspect of the church's vocation, beginning as individuals who challenge one another, and then involving the whole community: "'If another member of the church sins against you, go and point out the fault when the two of you are alone. If the member listens to you, you have regained that one. But if you are not listened to, take one or two others along with you, so that every word may be confirmed by the evidence of two or three witnesses'" (Matt. 18:15–16). An encounter like this might occur in a bar, as one confronts someone who's had too much to drink. It might take place in the stands of a Little League game, with another dad who questions why a mom volunteered to coach, or in an office where a colleague consistently has her contributions ignored. Or, in the church, it may mean noticing and addressing the man who lingers in the receiving line and comments on the pastor's legs but never her sermons.

To enter into community is to submit to one another in this particular way. We assent to the accountability that comes with belonging to one another, and this means that there will be occasional (perhaps even regular) conflict as we grow together into the likeness of Christ. If I am not willing to challenge someone in the interest of deconstructing patriarchy that harms both men and women, to pursue the justice that characterizes the kin-dom of God, then what, exactly, is worth the hard work of disagreement, of conflict, of challenge? Most of us will not play the role of Donald Trump on that *Access Hollywood* tape. But most of us will be in the shoes of Billy Bush, and in those moments we will be given the opportunity to cast our lot with Jesus, come what may.

## WATCH YOUR MOUTH

Even after years of working to use inclusive language—about God, especially—I still find myself slipping gendered language into places where it does not belong. Language is not everything. We have focused quite a bit on what we say, what words are off-limits, what someone said that they shouldn't have that compromises the platform they have in our culture. But you can say all the right words and still do damage through policy. Politicians can use the right rhetoric and still pass legislation that compromises access to health care for women, for example, and we can use inclusive language in our liturgy but still marginalize the voices of women in our places of worship. In this way, so much of our focus on language has occupied attention and used energy that might be more usefully oriented in the direction of patriarchal systems that make more of a tangible difference in the lives of women.

While that is true, words are also not nothing. Words create worlds, as Abraham Joshua Heschel said. His daughter, Susannah, recounted:

> Words, he often wrote, are themselves sacred, God's tool for creating the universe, and our tools for bringing holiness—or evil—into the world. He used to remind us that the Holocaust did not begin with the building of crematoria, and Hitler did not come to power with tanks and guns; it all began with uttering evil words, with defamation, with language and propaganda. Words create worlds, he used to tell me when I was a child. They must be used very carefully. Some words, once having been uttered, gain eternity and can never be withdrawn. The Book of Proverbs reminds us, he wrote, that death and life are in the power of the tongue.[3]

The way men talk about women matters, even when we think we can separate what we say from what we do. If you sexualize women in the way you talk to other men, this is the internal world you create, and the lens through which you will see. If you disregard women in conversation with other men, you will struggle to take them seriously in the world you share. We have a whole lexicon for words that assign negative connotations to the same qualities we might celebrate in men. Women are shrill, men are powerful; women are bossy, men are commanding; women are sluts, men are ladies' men; women are emotional, men are passionate. All of these cultivate something other than an understanding of the dignity of the women around us, instead reinforcing gender stereotypes and marginalizing women in "male" spaces.

Likewise, the words we use to describe our experience of God matter; when we use masculine language where gendered language is unnecessary, we create worlds where God is remade in our patriarchal image. I have known too many men who find the work of using inclusive language awkward and artificial and are unwilling to unlearn their patterns of speech in exchange for healthier (and more accurate) ones. Sometimes it does feel awkward to refer to God without using gender pronouns. Sometimes I feel I must choose how big a deal I make about calling God "she" because this may be the place the listener stops hearing what else is said. Ultimately, however, this is just laziness, an unwillingness to take the work of speaking about God as the heavy responsibility it is. If we believe that human life is to be valued and respected and protected, then using language that does not discriminate or exclude is paramount. This is about the gospel, about the work of justice Jesus came to do, as Dr. Lisa Davison reminds us:

> Without voices and often unnamed, women and other "outsiders" are excluded from human realms of power but certainly not from God's love. . . . Gospel words should not exclude anyone from knowing God's love and grace. Rather, amid a broken world, Christians must speak into being a new reality of God's reign where all are welcome.[4]

If learning to speak about God with precision and with a mind for justice and inclusion is strenuous, then that tells us something about the patterns that have shaped us, and how far they are from the truth of the God we know. However, this is work worth doing, work that matters, because it shapes how we see God and how we see the world.

Lastly, if nothing else, I hope this project is about telling the truth. To that end, all of us—including me—should admit that we have much work to do in the areas I have described, and much more. I have heard so many men voice their desire to create "a better world for their daughters" or wives or mothers, when addressing issues of sexual violence, inequality, and discrimination. I suppose whatever experience it takes for men to be convinced that women are people, human beings created in the image of God who should not have to live in the toxic bubble of patriarchy, is ultimately for the better. But you do not have to be motivated by your relationship to any particular woman to dismantle the patriarchal structure of the world in which we live. You need only believe in the world God created, in the relationships Jesus came to remake, in the vibrant communities the Spirit of God has called into existence. I have a wife, a sister, a mother, an aunt, nieces, sisters-in-law, many women who are dear to me; but I also have sons I hope will be freed from the versions of masculinity and femininity our culture has peddled. I hope they will not have to unlearn so many of the ways of seeing themselves and others that the patriarchy has formed. I hope they will be free to know themselves and to know others, to explore the fullness of their humanity, to have relationships of mutuality that make themselves and their partners the best versions of themselves they can be, so that they may serve God and their neighbors.

There is so much more beauty, so much more nuance, so much more to be explored apart from the false polarities we have made ourselves, apart from the value we have assigned them. The fullness of God is on display in our varied experiences of being; what holiness, what sacred things we miss when we shove some aside.

# Straight, White, and Female
## A Tangled Web of Oppression and Hope

MELISSA FLORER-BIXLER

### 1

My nine-year-old son reaches for my hand as we take our morning walk around the neighborhood. I mark the moment, calculate the feeling in my hand, the color of the sunrise on this morning, the temperature of the air, and the sounds of the birds. I want to remember. I know that we are reaching the end of such moments. The shame of this affection will find its way to him, one way or another.

### 2

A man meets me to discuss his recent break from complementarianism. His previous church taught him that his wife was subordinate to him, created to provide support and care for him. He was told that her subordination was woven into nature. It was in the fabric of his being to lead, pray, and act. She would follow, listen, and respond. They were suffocating under the contradiction of their lives, their daily partnership and mutual care smothered under an ideal they could not achieve. And eventually they realized there was nothing to achieve, only power working its way into the intimate places they treasured, warping what was given as a gift and rest.

He tells me this is the first time he has met with a woman alone in public. We are at a coffee shop surrounded by students pecking at laptops and coworkers trading office gossip. I had forgotten to be ashamed but then I feel the burn in my cheeks. I forgot that my body is suspicious here before others.

## 3

On November 5, 1918, Ruby Rogers stood before the three Black men in her yard who'd been brought for identification. Rogers claimed that a week before she'd been raped by a Black man who entered her home while her husband was in town, knocking her to the floor, along with her newborn baby.

After Rogers could not identify her assailant, tensions grew in the white community. Facing pressure to name her attacker, Rogers identified George Taylor, a Black farmer who had been visiting a friend in Rolesville on the day of the alleged assault. As Taylor was escorted to the local jail, a car carrying hooded assailants pulled up beside the police.

Taylor was taken to a ravine near Rogers's home, where he was shot more than a hundred times. A mob of more than three hundred white people gathered to participate in the lynching. White people took bullets home as souvenirs.

During the period of Reconstruction's failure that opened the steel jaws of Jim Crow, white women like me weaponized the frailty assigned to our bodies for the work of white supremacy. We welcomed getting ahead in white patriarchy, even if it meant making stepping stones out of the lives of Black and Brown people, crushing them on our way upward.

4

On the day that George Floyd is murdered, his neck crushed under a cop's knee, Christian Cooper searches for scarlet tanagers in Central Park. The bird-watcher is startled by a barking dog, unleashed in the wooded park. The dog's owner, Amy Cooper, runs after her cocker spaniel. Christian Cooper tells the woman to follow park regulations that require keeping the dog on a leash.

In anger, Amy Cooper dials the New York Police Department. "An African American man is threatening my life," she lies to the 911 dispatcher.

My white, female-gendered body is a testimony to the intersecting oppressions and hopes for liberation that are possible within systems of power that operate our world. All the powers of destruction and death are intertwined. Queer oppression is patriarchal oppression, a way to reinforce the gender hierarchy we have woven into our cultural, social, and legal systems. Racial power works to pit white women against women of color, convincing white women that our best hope is to eat the crumbs from the table of white men. Classism rewards certain forms of female experience (childbearing women married to men) as a stabilizing social force for the benefit of racialized patriarchy. Patriarchy reinforces its power by claiming a category of maleness that reifies itself at the cost of men's lives and well-being.

All of our oppressions are linked. Because of that, the hope of our thriving is knit together. The work of intersectional feminism and womanism make visible the webs of power that sustain certain forms of life even as they destroy others. We learn from bell hooks, Angela Y. Davis, and Ada María Isasi-Díaz that we untangle one part of this web until we are ready to be rid of it all. When we begin to pull at one oppression, we will begin to unravel the world as we have known it.

This also means our flourishing is bound together. Feminism is not a movement to place women above men in our social order any more than Black Lives Matter is an attempt to invert a racial hierarchy. Feminists want to free all of us from binary gendered categories. We want to make room for something new, knowing in our bones that there is no freedom until everyone is free. That freedom extends to men, who can be liberated from the stifling power of masculine essentialism.

And while this is good news, it is also frightening. What is left when the forms of life, the ways we have sustained society are no longer available? Freedom is unstable. It requires of us to let go of what we knew and to open ourselves to creating something else, and that "something" only comes to be in absence.

For people who follow Jesus, this will sound familiar. The Gospels offer us story after story of a Jesus who destabilizes the assumed foundations of social and cultural power that operated in first-century Palestine. He shares water at the well of a Samaritan woman. Jesus places the poor at the center of meals, challenging the logic of the patron-client system. He calls people to question family as their primary loyalty. Jesus interrogates the logic of religious power-keeping.

People are offended by this Jesus because he causes them to lose their bearings. There are ways of life they've come to rely on to give order to their world. And Jesus throws in a wrench by disrupting the patterns and assumptions that order their lives. I suspect that's why we read in John 6 that the crowds following Jesus go back to whatever they were doing before. They put up with the last disruption and return to their homes and their families, go back to the routines of culture and social formation that give life its predictability.

A few are left. Jesus asks them, "'Do you also wish to go away?'" We hear the response from Peter as a question. "'Lord, to whom can we go? You have the words of eternal life'" (John 6:67–68).

We are not given a description of what happens next. Jesus' followers will live out the words and acts of the Gospels in messy, complicated ways that often yield more failure and fighting than redemption. Then they will try again. I suspect that we will see a great deal of ourselves here, yielding our lives to the unpredictability of freedom from the categories of race, gender, and sexuality that order everything we do. In their place is a group of people unmoored from all but an insistence that God is making a new way, providing each day what we need to participate in the renewed creation.

# 8

## *Know Better, Do Better*

What kind of people commit to work that will have the consequence of drastically changing life for themselves, making it more complex and less comfortable? Who takes apart the house they live in, brick by brick, putting their own space in the world at risk? Put simply, those who are committed to the way of Jesus do this kind of work. Jesus of Nazareth was put to death and in the process exposed injustice that denied the sacred worth of all God's people.

The way churches talk about atonement (how Jesus' death on the cross brings about human salvation) often obscures this element of the gospel story, and for good reason—it would be disruptive to the economy of patriarchal white supremacy both inside and outside the church if we connected the call of discipleship to the forces that put Jesus to death. Any theory of the atonement that suggests God "needed" Jesus to die, or "sent" Jesus to die, obscures the deeply human political forces that put Jesus on the cross. Jesus was executed as a political subversive, and he was an enemy of both the state and those within the religious community who had shaped their religious identity to support and maintain the state's power. He was (and is) a threat precisely because he exposed the way inequality and power organized in empires and religious institutions had become weapons that elevated some while leaving others desperate for healing, for food, for inclusion in their communities, for wholeness. The deeper we go into cosmic theories of atonement that obscure the lived reality of Jesus' life and death, the more we separate Jesus from the context in which he lived; and if we separate Jesus from the context in which he lived, we spare ourselves the confrontation between the way of Jesus and our own lives together here and now.

I tell my congregation to be suspicious when they hear a generic Jesus offered to them; often, stripping Jesus of his particular human identity and disregarding the power dynamics of the culture he lived in serve a particular agenda for those who are interested in preserving things as they are. In his book *Reconstructing the Gospel: Finding Freedom from Slaveholder Religion,* Jonathan Wilson-Hartgrove writes, "There is no way to preach the gospel without proclaiming that the unjust systems of this world must give way to the reign of a new King."[1] In our history, we have preached something, but not the full gospel.

Samaritans, women, tax collectors, the sick, the blind, the paralyzed—in his encounters with them, Jesus exposed how the political and religious systems functioned to keep them on the margins. Over and over he made this exposure his work, calling powerful people to account, inviting people to come along, and always making it clear that this call is not about self-preservation but about becoming partners with God in building a more just and peaceable kin-dom among all people. To be a follower of Jesus means that you may be called to tear down the house you are living in, brick by brick, if indeed this is what is necessary for the machines of oppression to begin to falter. As if we could deny it, Jesus himself continued to expose these patterns of use and abuse until it cost him his very life. He preferred to die rather than to be silent or complacent in the face of the suffering of God's people. If we believe he had a choice—that his death on the cross was a decision to relinquish the power and privilege of being the Son of God and to be subject to the human forces of violence, injustice, and death—then we have at the center of our faith the example of One whose witness is that the liberation of God's people is worth our very lives.

This is why a theology that teaches us that Jesus made the ultimate sacrifice *on our behalf*—so that we wouldn't have to— is suspiciously convenient and ignores the many demands Jesus often made on his disciples, that they follow his example. A Christian theology that focuses primarily on the individual, and not the individual's relationship to the community at large, is not congruent with the larger narrative of Jesus' ministry and message. When Jesus exercises healing, often that healing is not about just physical restoration, but also restoring that person to belonging in the community. On the occasions that Jesus challenged the wealthy or those with authority, his invitation to repentance and ultimate discipleship was not only about "saving their souls" but also about doing justice by discipling the powerful. This is one of the ways Jesus saves us, by impelling us from lives of inaction and indifference to the committed work of doing justice in the world.

## RECONSTRUCTING WHITE, STRAIGHT MASCULINITY

Having deconstructed a particular worldview, we must go about the work of reconstructing an alternative in its place, or there will only ever be resistance where there might have been real transformation. No human being, regardless of how culpable they may be in the suffering and oppression of others, willingly leaves behind a worldview without the articulation of one found to be more appealing.

Consider other, more benign, bad habits. For years I bit my nails but had no incentive to change that habit until I made a pledge of solidarity with my kids, who were giving up thumb sucking. It was worth the effort because I could see an outcome

I desired. I came to this realization while potty training my children as well. There was no progress to be made until the new way was preferable to the old way (and this took much more convincing than one would think).

Much has been written and offered in the vein of deconstructing whiteness and patriarchy, and the destruction wrought on the world because of both should be enough reason to motivate change. However, deeply entrenched habits are not often overcome without new habits that meet the needs the old ones did, but in a more productive way.

There is a more abundant life to be found by doing the hard work of unlearning whiteness, toxic masculinity, and the like, but this is difficult to trust in a world so carefully constructed to preserve these ideals, a world that has so carefully conditioned us to depend on them. We have not grasped the mystery of what Jesus meant when he said that those who are willing to lose their lives will find them. To leave behind racial blindness is to leave behind a particular way of being and find liberation from the way white supremacy entraps the moral, spiritual self and makes us complicit in a system that does harm to the land and to Black and Brown bodies. To leave a patriarchal mindset behind is to leave behind attitudes, habits, and postures that minimize what does not fit the masculine/feminine binary, and to find the true selves that lie beneath these concepts of what it means to be "straight" or a "man."

The church seems to be uniquely equipped to form this kind of imagination. We are stewards of the scriptural story, which demonstrates both humanity's capacity for creating systems that marginalize a particular group of people and also God's deliberate and insistent intervention in human history to tear down those systems. However, without a destination on the horizon, we soon long for the familiarity of this spiritual bondage rather than the strange land of promise that God has in store. To that end, in this chapter, my hope is to draw on the spiritual imagination the Bible gives us to articulate what this journey with confession as our origin may look like.

## YOU HAVE TO WANT TO BE HEALED

On the journey away from the lie of patriarchal white supremacy are many, many places where it will be easier to turn back.
In John 5, Jesus encounters a man by the healing pool of Bethsaida. Tradition held that an angel would descend and stir
up the waters, and the first person to enter the pool would
be healed. For thirty-eight years the man had lived with his
disability, and yet Jesus asks him, "'Do you want to be made
well?'" This seems to be a ridiculous question. Of course he
does! In a culture where having a disability carries so much
social stigma, so much isolation, and so many physical challenges, surely he does not prefer lying by that pool, hoping
against hope that he might be able to walk again.

However, the question Jesus asks does not imply just well-
ness, but wholeness. "Do you want to be made whole?" is a
better translation. Wholeness, I think, is different from well-
ness. Wholeness has to do with a kind of completeness in your
life, the healing of things that may have broken your body or
fragmented your spirit. Your body can be well and your life
not be whole, because your spirit is broken—because of a fractured relationship or a sense of inadequacy or a simmering rage
at the senseless violence unleashing tragedy on innocent lives.
Likewise, your spirit can be well, while your body has particular limitations. There are all kinds of people living with all
kinds of limiting, painful conditions who possess more peace,
courage, and determination than the rest of us—indeed, who
would not change their bodies at all, despite what we may see
as limitations and imperfections. Jesus is talking about wholeness: the reconciliation of body and spirit, the just peace of all
living things, a kind of healing even deeper than the kind we
think we need.

Raj Nadella, a professor at Columbia Seminary, makes it
plain: at the pool is a system where there's equal access but
not equal opportunity.[2] Anybody can get in, but not *everybody* can get in. It could be that Jesus is wondering if this man

really thinks he can be whole, even if he gets in the water and is healed, but then gets up and leaves behind all those folks just like him, sitting there waiting the way he was. Can you be whole without *everyone* being whole? This connects deeply to privilege. Essentially, one without privilege is asking to experience it—to be gifted the ability to have his needs met, his healing granted, whether the others join him or not. Instead of working within this system, Jesus works around it.

Even if I can manage to benefit from a system to receive what I need or desire, I cannot be free if my neighbors are not free. The systems of whiteness and patriarchy exist for advantage, an advantage we apparently feel we need, so much so that we are willing to go to such varied (and often violent) lengths to protect it. The salvation Christ offers us is time and space where radically new relationships exist, where there is no need for advantage because of how deep and broad the presence of God's love and justice is in all of creation. Relinquishing the persistent fear and insecurity that drive our desire to have and to keep privilege is inherent in accepting the salvation Jesus offers us.

The question for us, then, is if we want to be made whole. This is harder work than getting "woke" or changing viewpoints or politics. It has little to do with how you respond to racist jokes or memes, or simply improving individual behavior toward others. It means confronting inconvenient truths, accepting that people in our lives who love us deeply have done us harm by passing on ideas that are destructive, accepting that we have done harm we cannot undo, and spending the rest of our lives unlearning habits ingrained in us by the culture in which we were born and raised. It means accepting that the real damage in America is not done so much by email forwards or off-color jokes, but by patriarchal white supremacy embedded in our economic, education, and criminal justice systems. The question is real and important: Do you want to be made whole? Do you want to live in a world that draws on the gifts of every person? Do you want to live in a country that faces its painful past rather than reliving it in every generation? Do you want to make your life about something other than proving your worth? We will have to answer again and again, as we are introduced to truths that are neither pleasant nor convenient and as we see how intricate the machinery that perpetuates these injustices really is.

## DISCOVER YOUR WORTH

The most basic commandment—the whole of the Law and the Prophets, Jesus said—is to love God with all your heart, soul, mind, and strength, and to love your neighbor as yourself. The scriptural story is full of humans' attempts to achieve security for themselves by acquiring wealth and land and subjugating others. The Israelites, from the moment of their liberation, struggled to trust that the God who brought them out of bondage in Egypt would sustain them through the wilderness. Often, what we hear in the story of the Hebrew people is a desire to become what they have been fighting—to be victor on the battlefield, to enlarge their territory, to have a king who sits on a throne. The answer to their fear that God may not, in fact, be with them, that the love of God may not after all be true, brought on by these traumas, is to secure themselves through other means.

White colonizers who came to America brought with them a deep and abiding sense of inadequacy. Many, we learned in elementary school, were fleeing religious persecution. They left a society that rejected them for who they were in order to create a land of religious freedom and liberty, but they sought to heal their trauma by becoming those who inflict trauma (consciously and unconsciously).

This is what we learn, from the earliest moments we are socialized on the playgrounds and in the hallways at school: there is a social hierarchy, and you do not want to be at the bottom of it. For that reason, your work is creating a reason why someone, anyone, should be below you on it. For kids, it adds up to shoes and jeans and a cool haircut. On a much grander, more elaborate, and more violent scale, patriarchal white supremacy is born out of this desire to avoid being on the bottom by putting those with more melanin or a different gender identity or sexual orientation there instead. But if you believe that grace is true; if you believe that you were created in the image of God; if you believe that you, along with all of creation, have been redeemed by Jesus of Nazareth, then why is this hierarchy necessary? God invites us to imagine another way.

Near the end of Isaiah, in chapter 65, Isaiah imagines a world no longer built on exploitation or consumption, a world where the thriving of some does not come at the expense of others, a world without fear of scarcity or isolation. In Deuteronomy, the promise of the land that God makes to Abraham, Isaac, and Jacob uses conquering language. It will be "a land with fine, large cities that you did not build, houses filled with all sorts of goods that you did not fill, hewn cisterns that you did not hew, vineyards and olive groves that you did not plant."[3] In other words, the sign of God's blessing (as articulated by people who had yet to experience victory) will be acquisition through destruction and invasion; it's when your gain is another's loss, when you are able to dominate another. By the time in which Isaiah is writing, the people of Judah have experienced both victory and defeat; they have experienced what it means for their homes and vineyards and land and labor to be the source of someone else's blessing. The people have seen domination swing back and forth; they have seen that the cycle of exploitation is not in keeping with the notion that all of us are created in the image of God, including those who have been pitted against one another as enemies. This vision from Isaiah is a depiction of an alternative, where there is equity and justice, where one's flourishing is not the result of another's suffering. In the kin-dom of God, one does not need to step on the neck of another to reach the heights of belovedness.

This is what those of us who call ourselves straight or white or male have not yet come to believe, at least not in such a way that we might order our lives around this truth. But let us call patriarchal white supremacy for what it is: an elaborate, violent, dehumanizing way to assure ourselves of what cannot be assured apart from God.

And so we must learn to embrace our belovedness, realizing that so much of the "strength" we show is often a poor attempt at filling a hole only the love of God can fill. We have seen this time and again: the way white men's sense of inadequacy fueled the image of the Black man as one to be feared, the way patriarchy established feminine attributes as pejoratives, out of fear that we would not be loved or protected by others bound by the same patriarchal mind-set. Part of the fragility of our humanity is a sometimes difficult and taunting uncertainty about who we are and who God made us to be, a willingness to accept something less than the life God has promised for us, a nagging and sometimes paralyzing doubt about the gifts God has given us. The irony, of course, is that this doubt about our strength, our value, our beauty, is masked as arrogance and abuse. One who believes in the beauty of one's own sexuality does not need to demean another's. One who is comfortable with who they are in the sight of God has no need of treating another as less than human.

So many of us have spent our lives trying to prove ourselves because we never got approval from people in our lives who weren't equipped to give it. The toxic forms of masculinity we have practiced over generations have taught us to withhold our feelings, especially feelings of love and affection, in favor of toughness. If we raise our children in a way that makes our approval the prize they are always chasing, perhaps, we think, we will make them tough and motivate them at the same time. Instead, we create a wound, a nagging self-doubt that they will try to cover rather than heal. We make ourselves feel better— more powerful, more worthy, more capable—by diminishing others because they have different skin pigmentation or gender identity or sexual orientation. Ultimately, so much of the pain we have inflicted on others is a result of the anger we have about our own unresolved pain. The trauma that comes with being unsure of our worth, in the sight of God and others, is trauma we have chosen to pass on rather than heal. We have created systems to diminish others, and they are rooted in our own pain at how diminished we feel—because we have forgotten that God's love for us is not something we earn, but instead something we honor by building lives that reflect that love to those around us.

And no matter what affirmations you have or have not gotten in your life, the love of God is true. No matter where we go or who we're with, no matter who or what tries to tear us down or tempt us to a life other than the one God has in store for us, we are God's beloved, and we have been made to live lives of peace and mercy, to be surrounded by love and grace, to live in the fullness of relationship with God and with each other. Maybe you grew up in a house where people told you that, maybe your mom or dad leaned down to you in a moment where you might have wondered and made sure you knew. Or maybe not. Maybe you live in a perpetual state of wondering if who you are is good enough for anybody. If you are straight, white, and male, this doubt is our inheritance, buried so far down, deep in the habits and traditions of whiteness, maleness, and heteronormativity and all of their uses and abuses, that it seems ridiculous to suggest insecurity and doubt could be at the root. How is it that people who mostly walk around the world acting like they own it are actually in need of affirmation? Ultimately, if we are secure in the love God has for us, then we know that this love is not a finite resource, we have no need of diminishing anyone else, and we desire the liberation that comes with knowing this love for everyone else around us. Until we reckon with why we need women to be submissive, why we need persons of color to be inferior, and why we search the Bible looking for reasons to diminish our LGBTQ+ siblings in the family of God, we will have done immeasurable harm and still not satisfied what it is we are longing for.

This is one of the reasons we baptize people, and for that matter, one of the reasons the church exists—to be, in the midst of a world that is all too ready to convince us otherwise, a reminder for one another of God's love and affirmation for each one of us. Unfortunately, we have often betrayed this purpose. When Jesus said that the kin-dom of God is like a mustard seed, he described the mustard bush it becomes as a place where the birds of the air can make a nest, find a home. How many have come to the church for that kind of safety and affirmation, only to find rejection instead? To find careful descriptions of all the ways they are most unlovable, which are often not the things Jesus himself found unlovable? You can know that God loves you and believes in you, but sometimes you need to hear it.

You need to know that God's love is not dependent on the world's measures of success and failure, that it is not even dependent on your succeeding or failing in serving God. Why withhold this good news from one another? In Romans, Paul asks what can separate us from the love of Christ. Can persecution or nakedness or famine or peril or sword; can life or death or things present or things to come, can angels or rulers, can anything else in all creation? No, he says. None of these.[4]


## BE DIFFERENT

Another of the reasons we baptize people is to forge an identity strong enough to resist the ones the rest of the world will constantly try to ascribe to us. To be a straight man who has no need for the toxic brands of masculinity in our culture, to be a white person without the need for the trappings of whiteness, is to be an outlier in the wider culture in which we live. It's possible—even likely—that deconstructing particular ways of thinking and living will alter relationships that have been profoundly important in our lives. I suppose this is what Jesus meant when he said that he came not to bring peace but a sword, to set those who might be family against one another (Matt. 10:34–36). Growing deeper in our discipleship, desiring greater faithfulness to the way of Jesus, will ultimately mean that our relationships with those for whom this is a problem will be changed, perhaps ended.

In the letter to the church at Philippi, Paul urges the believers there to "let the same mind be in you that was in Christ Jesus" (Phil. 2:5), the mind of a servant who relinquishes privilege, as I argue in chapter 1. In the next chapter, Paul makes a simple but profound statement: "Our citizenship is in heaven" (3:20). This verse is the inspiration for Stanley Hauerwas and William Willimon's foundational work, *Resident Aliens*.[5] We live here, but who we are may make us strangers in this place. The church, they argue, is "an outpost, an island of culture in the middle of another" where a particular set of values is learned and practiced, even though those virtues may be in conflict with the surrounding culture.[6] This makes us nonconformists. And from the very moment when we became self-aware social creatures, we have each learned that there is security in belonging, we can derive value from belonging, and there is a cost associated with not belonging.

One of my children recently entered middle school, and he asked me questions about that time in my own life. These were not all fond memories. I arrived in sixth grade as a somewhat sheltered kid whose musical tastes, wardrobe, and haircut did not exactly help me fit into my environment, and I heard about it. To add to it, I played in the band and made good grades— a lethal combination for adolescent social standing. I hadn't gone to elementary school with many of my middle school classmates, and therefore didn't have a built-in friend group (thank goodness for the one good friend I did have). Nothing I liked was the popular thing to like. By seventh grade, some of the kids learned that I could hang with them in their pickup basketball games on the blacktop, and I found a place in the social strata. Perhaps the most comforting thing was that I now had a group of friends—a community within the larger community that provided a kind of acceptance and protection I didn't feel before. It's a vulnerable time in our lives, and it's the time when we become keenly aware of the cost that comes with being different. (Of course, it is true that anyone with a skin tone or gender expression that is outside the majority experiences this much earlier and with much greater risk.)

We like to think we grow out of this stage, and perhaps we do to a degree, but we carry this need for acceptance into adulthood. No one really enjoys wearing a necktie; we do it because it's what's required to be taken seriously in certain settings. I won't begin to presume I know all of the things women in our culture are forced to change about themselves in order to find a partner or be taken seriously in the workplace (or in the church), but I do feel confident in saying that list is a long one.

We all have limits when it comes to the social consequences we are willing to accept in exchange for standing on our principles and the compromises we are willing to make in order to be accepted and to feel as if we belong. In order to construct the kind of life that takes our discipleship seriously, and to be straight white men who desire justice above all else, we must be prepared to face social (as well as material) consequences we have perhaps not been willing to accept to this point.

One of the consequences we must learn to accept is occasional loneliness. Even among "progressive" straight white men, there is the version of ourselves we present to the world, which we believe is required of us in order to be accepted in circles where an understanding of race, sex, and gender issues is a kind of social currency. Many of us exist in these circles, in conversations with women, with persons of color, with LGBTQ+ friends, and have a heightened awareness of what is required of us. However, few of us operate only in those circles. We also find ourselves in relationships with those who assume that because we look like we do, we share particular assumptions and values. Each of us makes small decisions all the time about how much trouble we are willing to cause when we find ourselves in a place where it may cost us to demonstrate that we value something different.

Going deeper in one's discipleship, growing closer to the Jesus who works for justice among and on behalf of the marginalized, often means that our relationships with those who do not share that pursuit must change. While they may not cease to exist, it is difficult to maintain close relationships, even to feel welcome, among a group of people when you are so clearly in the minority in such a fundamental way. Hauerwas and Willimon say this beautifully: anyone "who dares to speak the truth among a people of falsehood will be lonely. But this is loneliness, solitude, for the right reasons. Jesus was often alone and lonely. His loneliness was a function of his prophetic holiness; he was often alone among people because he was a friend of God."[7]

The temptation is to believe that if we are evolving as people in such a way that relationships end or change, or we begin making significant lifestyle changes, something must be wrong—we are taking it too far. The truth is that we are always alienated in some way from our neighbors. Either we are living in patterns that support or perpetuate the status quo, and we exist in broken relationships with those whose suffering is tied to our being more comfortable, or we are making enemies of those who believe we have given in to political correctness in all its forms by deconstructing the habits of patriarchal whiteness they do not see as a problem. If we begin with clarity about this choice, perhaps choosing which is preferable becomes easier. To make peace with having enemies and reconstruct who we are apart from patriarchal white supremacy, we must make peace with making enemies for the right reasons.

This is especially true for clergy, who must frequently choose how they present the gospel of Jesus to a people who expect that gospel to be tailored to their lives as they are, even to their prejudices as they are. When I was a seminarian and working as an intern for the Rev. Barber, I shared my fear that if I had the deeply communal and justice-oriented ministry I was being taught to practice, I might not be employed in ministry very long. His response has stayed with me all these years. "Well, you know," he said, "Isaiah is a long book, but Amos is a short one."

Preachers make calculations—how can I preach the radical Jesus I find in the text in such a way that I might be heard, even by someone inclined to reject the present-day connections the text invites, while also being true to the text? And how long and how hard can I push, until my leadership in this community is ultimately rejected?

This weekly tightrope can be so difficult to walk because so many of our people believe that our primary responsibility is to make them feel good, or better. Because the church is as market-driven as any other entity in America, those who are dissatisfied or disappointed or simply reject the notion that the gospel of Jesus might challenge so much of what it means to be American can go down the street to a different church and a different pastor who is content to tell them what they want to hear when we make them angry or disappoint them.

The clergyperson—especially the straight white male clergyperson—must learn to live without the love and admiration that come from a congregation that thinks they can do no wrong, even as the ego thirsts for those things. It is frighteningly easy to chase this praise, even unconsciously. This is loneliness of a different sort. One of the great blessings of congregational ministry is the relationships clergy build with those they walk alongside. If we maintain enough distance in our own hearts and minds between ourselves and those people to be able to tell them a truth they may find objectionable, we are never really free to let down our guards. The implication is that we spend a great deal of our time building relationships that must, by nature, include enough distance to accommodate the demands of prophetic ministry. That can be lonely, and it can mean rejection, which means faithfulness must be more desirable than praise.

For as much as deconstructing patriarchal white supremacy in our lives may cost us, there is no way to quantify the grace inherent in the new community it makes possible. Few of us realize just how much our identities shape our relationships with others who do not look like us or identify as we do. There are walls that exist between us, necessitated by a legacy of physical, spiritual, and emotional violence. This wall is described beautifully, poetically, by Ta-Nehisi Coates in *Between the World and Me*. We are so frequently oblivious to the posture that those who do not fit the ideals of patriarchal white supremacy take around us as a means of self-preservation. As a result, we are also ignorant of what happens on the other side of the wall, what beauty and love we are missing, until that wall comes down, or we get a glimpse on the other side.

We had a chance to see the other side in the flood of book groups and conversations around race that sprung up in the wake of George Floyd's murder in 2020. Books on race and whiteness surged in sales. Police brutality was not a new phenomenon, and institutionalized racism in policing and other aspects of American life weren't new either. But books like Austin Channing Brown's *I'm Still Here: Black Dignity in a World Made for Whiteness* and Coates's *Between the World and Me* and Ibram X. Kendi's *How to Be an Antiracist* hold up a mirror that allows white people to see themselves through the eyes of Black Americans demanding that their lives be honored and their voices heard. At least part of white fascination with this genre is the intrigue of learning how we are perceived by others. This knowledge is not necessarily enough to precipitate change, but it does make it possible.

I have been able to build relationships that have allowed me to see deeper authenticity on the part of someone who might otherwise (out of necessity) be guarded around someone like me. This does not mean that they are sure that I will do no harm; in fact, it is likely that I will, because I cannot always see or understand. What those relationships have allowed me to see is that I do not wish to have the kind of relationships where I am closed off from knowing and being known in the fullest way possible by those around me. It reflects a basic theological truth: we were made for fellowship with God and with one another. The journey of faith we are on is about learning what it means to be closer to both; in fact, for those of us who follow Jesus of Nazareth, who put love of God and love of neighbor in the same plane, we cannot love one without loving the other.

There is so much meaning and purpose to be found in deep relationship, so much of God's presence for our lives. Deconstructing identities that keep us from living into the fullness of those relationships, while difficult, is also a profound gift. Because we can know and be known, and this is what we are all longing for in this life.

If this deconstruction costs us certain relationships, or our place in particular communities, it also makes possible new community around the shared values of discipleship. There are the families we are born into and then there are the families that the Spirit of God calls together. I have gathered at the Lord's Table with so many whose stories I have come to know, who have come to be outcasts and outliers in their own families because their relationship with Jesus and their study of Scripture and their experience of community have alienated them from the families into which they were born. In those moments, that Table is a family table, a table around which they gather with those who know them, love them, and embrace them, not because of shared blood or history, but because the love of God has brought them there. I can see the faces of those for whom Jesus has not meant peace but a sword, a dividing line in relationships on which many of us rely. But here, we get new siblings and new parents, new grandparents and new children, and the common bond between us is profound. Hauerwas and Willlmon are right that following Jesus makes us a stranger to some people, places, and circumstances—but the church (at its best) is God's healing gift for the loneliness we may experience.

People who eat, pray, and pursue justice together, who share joys and struggles together, who walk with one another over time, encounter the presence of God at every turn. Theirs are lives with profound meaning and purpose, and they are living the "eternal" life Jesus talked about. We tend to think of time in a linear sense—there is past, there is present, there is future—and eternal life is the life we will have when this one is over. But to speak of the eternal in the way Jesus describes it is to participate in something that always has been, is now, and always will be. He has given us the opportunity to define our lives by something beyond the confines of birth and death, something larger than our own lives, something that reaches as far into the past as it does into the future. The pursuit of this life, eternal life with Christ, seems a worthwhile reason to leave behind an old one; indeed, reason enough to move quickly from reluctance to joy.

# Multiply Marginalized

## Living Life in the Fragments

ROBYN HENDERSON-ESPINOZA

I live life in the fragments, in the interstices, in the spaces in between, because I am born of a Mexican woman not of this country, am a nonbinary transgender Latinx, live life as an openly queer person, and live on the autism spectrum. I live in the fragments of my own becoming.

I do know what it's like to live in the whole pieces; I watched it before my eyes when I was in college at a small Baptist university in West Texas. Hardin-Simmons University taught me that my questions weren't for the classroom. The classroom was for serious questions and inquiry, questions that came from white male-bodied students. I learned that my place was to be quiet, to silence my queries and acquiesce to the cisheteropatriarchy of the culture. I learned that I wasn't good at acquiescing and that my questions destabilized the reigning epistemology. I was never good at being part of the whole; I only knew and still only know how to be on the outside, in the fragments of life. I learned that there is life in the fragments, in the borderlands of becoming, in the shadows of the whole pieces that are the dominant culture.

Learning to navigate race, class, gender, sexuality, and ability as an *other* is not an easy task, especially when you're also navigating Southern Baptist life. I learned to read alone, unsupervised, finding books and articles to inform my study because so much of the classroom was composed of supremacist thought, and because my questions were too far outside the scope of what my professors understood as Christian life. The exceptions were two cisgender, white, male professors who encouraged me to pursue graduate study with a Latin American Baptist theologian, a woman. These two professors, with whom I am still connected, became my lifeline in the field of theology and ethics. They nurtured my questions and breathed life into the fragments.

The scandal of me leaving the patriarchy of Texas, my roots, was my own leaning into the fragments of a life that I was still piecing together as a first-generation college graduate. I learned how to pay attention to the bodies of others who were in class with me—men, mainly, who were the ones pursuing ordination. But there in Chicago, I found my voice.

The voice of *otherness*, the voice of *nepantla* (the in-between spaces), is the voice that I embrace these days as someone who lives in a body that is multiply marginalized. My gender-nonconforming trans body is a body of difference, comprised of fragments from the Red River of Texas down to the valley of the Rio Grande, crossing multiple times the Mississippi River, leaning into the queer utopia of the Bay Area, and finally criss-crossing, again, these United States to make my home in Nashville, Tennessee. My body, my voice, my vocation is comprised of the fragments of my own becoming.

Learning to navigate the privilege of others meant that I needed to understand my own standpoints. What does it mean to be born of a Mexican woman not of this country but to have the ability to navigate higher education and earn a doctor of philosophy in constructive philosophical theology and philosophical ethics? It means that I hold privilege in my body, too, and I must learn how to compost that privilege and live responsibly in a way that creates conditions of possibility for a sustainable life for those around me. Learning to navigate both oppression and privilege also means that I must learn how to build relationships that afford me conditions to live out my vocation in a way that doesn't accelerate unprocessed trauma. After all, every bit of oppression is unprocessed trauma, and I've seen enough unprocessed trauma to last me a lifetime. I navigate oppression, practice boundary making every day with those who move through the world seamlessly with no issue, and turn inward to care for myself as best as I'm able given that I live life in the fragments of my own becoming.

When I was introduced to Kimberlé Crenshaw's work on intersectionality, I began to understand the impact of my life in the fragments. I began to understand the complexities of my own becoming, and I began to lean into the path of what the politics of radical difference might invite me to sojourn. Intersectionality, a legal theory designed to show the ways in which the rule of law is inherently biased and racist against Black women, specifically, became a guiding light for me as I sought to suture the wounds of my own becoming and try to turn the fragments of my own life into an afghan studded with touchstones that were intelligible not only to me but also to the world around me. I sought to draw parallels between my life as a wandering nomad searching for meaning in a whitened cisheteropatriarchal world, so that my fragments were contoured with the beauty of my becoming, not encumbered with the overwhelming oppression that I watched during my childhood. This work of becoming is harder than I thought; I am still becoming.

Being multiply marginalized in a world that seeks to flatten out my differences means that I must always lift up the fragments, however broken they are, so that I might find wholeness with others who are also living life in the fragments. I think here of immigrants, the poor, differently abled persons, transgender persons, queer persons, and many others who find themselves fragmented and cut up into little pieces disposed of in a world that only wants pristine, white, cisgender, able-bodied men. Being a person who holds multiple standpoints that are often silenced by the dominant culture means that I must compost the bullshit and do the necessary inner work, so that my outer work reflects the deep spiritual practices of changing myself to change the world.

Multiply marginalized people are most often ignored and silenced, as I once was when I was a young theology student at Hardin-Simmons University. The courage of those two cisgender male-bodied professors, who risked being called liberals, created conditions for me to be in relationship with difference—the difference of myself and the difference of the world. Sometimes relationships save us from ourselves, from the unprocessed trauma that accelerates multisystem oppressions. Learning to navigate my own fragments, so that I might be fully alive and participate in my own becoming, however fraught it was with difficulty, poverty, and oppression, all comes back to the relationships I had with two cisgender, white, able-bodied professors in college. Their leaning into relationship with me helped me lean into relationship with myself. These fractal moments created conditions for me to live a full life from the place of the fragments and to participate in my own becoming in such a way that I now translate theory to action and theology to praxis. I couldn't have seen myself outside of these two relationships with my college professors, and I couldn't have become the theologian I am today outside of studying with a Latin American Baptist theologian.

As I am often reminded by and through my inner work, *I am still becoming,* and this becoming hasn't been easy, nor has it been simple. Navigating my own difference in a world that doesn't want me to thrive and shuts me out of processes that only invite the dominant culture means that I am still navigating the fragments of my life and the reality of supremacy culture.

When I found my voice as a theologian and ethicist, I found the smoothest parts of my fragmented life, though not without complications. These fragments are the most beautiful pieces of my work, calling me into deeper folds of my own becoming. Navigating multiple marginalizations means that I must be very clear on who I am. I am grateful that relationships continue to teach me who I am and who I am becoming.

# Conclusion

What do you see when you look in the mirror? In your Twitter bio—where there is limited space and the pressure to be succinct, descriptive, and maybe a little witty—what do you write? Is our identity primarily a question of how we define ourselves, or are our lives defined by how they are lived in relation to others? For me, these are unresolved questions with complex answers. As I said in the introduction, one of the things that motivated this book was my realization of the apparent gap between how I perceive myself and how others perceive me. Only I am privy to my inner monologue, the narrative that shapes my life, and the way I see myself is shaped by much, much more than what the world sees me do or hears me say. However, I live in a body, and that body, as Dr. Robyn Henderson-Espinoza described, carries with it certain associations that I may or may not wish to bear. As my desire to follow Jesus grows, as frustration with the injustice I see around me simmers, I want more and more for the world to see that version of me. I want to *be*, rather than to *seem*.

I want my identity to be a faithful intersection of the person I believe myself to be and the person the rest of the world experiences. I want to be a person who sees the suffering of those around me and is willing to do the work of understanding my place in that suffering. I want to be a person who raises children to do the same, to leave this world having given myself to the work of making it a more just, more loving place. And I want others to see little difference between the person I seem to be and the person I am. We are all, as Dr. Robyn wrote, becoming. No matter who I am becoming, that person will be flawed, but the grace of God allows me to wear my failures with humility and honesty, and to resist covering them over with the facades that have so frequently characterized whiteness and masculinity. I know that I am still on a journey of discovery and exploration, learning where I am in relation to where I want to be as a Christian, as a straight white male in a culture where those identities have wrought far too much pain and suffering.

"Who am I, and what am I becoming?" seem like the kind of existential questions straight white men do not frequently have to ask themselves. My hope is that we will be willing to think again about those questions, to invite new ways of thinking and being into our lives so that they are lived for a purpose other than holding onto power and privilege.

We cannot begin to love as God commanded us to love—indeed, to make our whole lives, our entire being, about this love—if we have not embraced the belovedness of all people. We have an easier time acknowledging the image of God in some as opposed to others. That acknowledgment cannot be solely intellectual or emotional. On this subject, we have great confusion. Many, many of us insist that the condition of our hearts and minds is pure, while the rhythm of our daily lives suggests something quite different. It is difficult for me to demonstrate love for my transgender siblings, for example, if I will not take the time to learn their preferred language, use desired pronouns, or seek justice for those who are disproportionately victims of violent crimes. In our churches, we use language that implies that all are welcome, in the interest of fashioning ourselves loving and accepting of everyone, but we have not asked ourselves why there are no LGBTQ+ members of our community.

Each of us knows that "love" is a verb, but too often we have defined it by what we do not do, instead of what we do. When someone shares the experience of being racially profiled, or a woman shares the experience of being objectified, perhaps it seems like the most loving thing is to do your best to avoid doing those things—but love is more active than passive and often involves intention more than restraint. The opportunity to respond in loving ways to the pain and injustice we see around us is an opportunity to discern where love requires our own transformation, for the sake of our neighbors; indeed, to allow ourselves to become allies in the sense that we are intent on addressing not only our own behaviors but also the systems that dehumanize our neighbors. Saying "I don't see color" (another way of saying that I try not to act on racial prejudice) is a way of defining one's response in the negative. In reality, I ignore a large part of how this person experiences the world in which we both live, and do nothing to address the lived reality of a person of color trying to survive in a society built on white supremacy. To love is to work actively in the interest of another, to sacrifice something of myself (even all of myself, in the case of Jesus) so that my neighbors are able to have a greater experience of God's presence in their lives. We cannot love our neighbors—our trans neighbors, gay neighbors, Indigenous neighbors—without making tangible changes to the world we all inhabit.

To that end, there is no such thing as someone else's struggle. If my being free (in Christ) is bound up in the liberation of others, then I must know what binds them and especially where I have a hand in it. The struggles of my neighbors, the dreams of my neighbors, become mine as well when my vocation is healing, serving, working as a partner with God in remaking the world. There will always be something new for me to learn, another person's story to know. In American culture, we have learned to prize what is ours, our own individual liberties, the rights we have to live as we see fit. We are free, in many ways, to make our own choices, but we are not free from the consequences of those choices. Across generations, the choice we have made to build and sustain patriarchal white supremacy has had disastrous effects for the lives of our neighbors, and this has led us to deeply divided, distrustful, alienated relationships with one another.

The way of Jesus will not allow us to live free while others are bound. We cannot be whole until others are too. And so Christ calls us to the vocation of servanthood, of lifting up those whose lives have been disrupted, whose sense of self-worth has been harmed, whose bodies have been violated, until just ways of living offer healing for these deep wounds. What would it mean if we spent less time thinking about our freedoms and spent more ensuring the liberation of our neighbors, who have waited far too long for us to stop standing in the way of their becoming who God has called them to be?

Here, perhaps, we will find the people we are becoming. Despite the toxic history we have inherited, perhaps God is equipping us to see the truth of the lie we have been told and to become those who help to pull up patriarchal white supremacy by its roots, so that the world God has promised can be born through us and not in spite of us. If we look around, we can see that many others have already been about this work. Now let us begin, and join them.

# Acknowledgments

When I told my kids I was going to write and publish this book, they had two questions. The first was if it would be dedicated to them (ever humble, they are) and the second was if it would mean I'd have less time to spend with them. The first I had already planned to oblige, and the second I did my best to answer "no," though they have surely sacrificed across the time it took for me to write (and rewrite). My hope is that as they grow older, they will find that this book is, in part, intended to be a gift to them and a way they might know their dad in a different way. My wife has perhaps made the greatest sacrifices, clearing time and opportunity for me to write—on retreats, family vacations, and more. She also managed to strike just the right balance of "how's the book coming?" with knowing when not to mention it, which requires a deft touch. Her challenge to me, as I noted in the introduction, was a large part of my motivation to write this book. She has made me a better man.

My family of origin has made countless jokes over the years about the book I needed to write, which have demonstrated a faith in me that, at times, felt outsized. We all need people who see what we can't see in ourselves and love us unconditionally, and my family has certainly been that for me. They've also expressed their hope that sales from the book would allow them all to retire. I hope their faith in me is rewarded even if their hopes for a life of luxury are dashed.

I am also grateful to my dear friend and colleague Erin Wathen, who has encouraged me to write more, given me helpful advice, shared her own platform, and connected me with Jessica Miller Kelley, the fantastic editor of this book, who has also been so encouraging, wise, and endlessly patient.

Without them, you wouldn't be reading this. In addition, the contributors to this book took a risk by agreeing to have their names lumped together with a straight white man and trusting that the work we would do here, together, would be worthwhile and faithful. Bishop Barber, Dr. Robyn, Melissa, Matthias: what a gift you have given all of us with your words in these pages.

Thank you to my EDB family for the deepest friendships life offers and to Barton, for creating space for unadulterated honesty and the deepest trust among friends. I owe thanks also to my friends outside ministry who have allowed me to be someone other than pastor since the earliest moments of this call on my life. You have—against all odds and any reasonable expectation—kept me balanced, and I am grateful for that.

And last but certainly not least, to Covenant Christian Church: thank you for the space you have given me to pursue this dream of mine, for abiding my tendency to push your buttons, for supporting me and cheering me on along the way, and for loving and supporting me and my family. I hold gratitude also for the prior churches I have served in Durham, in England, and in Alexandria, that you bore patiently with me as I evolved. Surely the evolution was not all pleasant!

With gratitude for what has been and an abiding hope for what might be—

The Rev. Chris Furr
September 2021
Cary, North Carolina

# Notes

## Chapter 1: The Lie Beneath

1. Amanda Barroso and Anna Brown, "Gender Pay Gap in U.S. Held Steady in 2020," Pew Research Center, May 25, 2021, https://www.pewresearch.org/fact-tank/2021/05/25/gender-pay-gap-facts/.

2. Howard Thurman, *Jesus and the Disinherited* (Boston: Beacon Press, 1976), 2.

3. James Baldwin, "As Much Truth as One Can Bear," *New York Times,* January 14, 1962, https://www.nytimes.com/1962/01/14/archives/as-much-truth-as-one-can-bear-to-speak-out-about-the-world-as-it-is.html.

## Chapter 2: "Queer" Is Not a Four-Letter Word

1. Daniel Erlander, *Manna and Mercy: A Brief History of God's Unfolding Promise to Mend the Entire Universe* (Mercer Island, WA: Order of Saints Martin and Teresa, 1992), vi.

2. Mark D. Jordan, *The Invention of Sodomy in Christian Theology* (Chicago: University of Chicago Press, 1997), 1.

3. Jared Yates Sexton, *The Man They Wanted Me to Be: Toxic Masculinity and a Crisis of Our Own Making* (Berkeley, CA: Counterpoint, 2019), 73.

4. Sexton, 144.

5. Sexton, 139.

6. Sexton, 184.

7. Meg-John Barker and Julia Scheele, *Queer: A Graphic History* (London: Icon Press, 2016), 19.

8. Barker and Scheele, 20.

9. Casey E. Copen, Anjani Chandra, and Isaedmarie Febo-Vazquez, "Sexual Behavior, Sexual Attraction, and Sexual Orientation among Adults Aged 18–44 in the United States: Data from the 2011–2013 National Survey of Family Growth," *National Health Statistics*

*Reports* 88 (January 7, 2016): 7–10, https://www.cdc.gov/nchs/data/nhsr/nhsr088.pdf.

10. Rachel Gurevich, "Using Transgender Youths' Chosen Names May Lower Suicide Risk," Reuters, April 10, 2018, https://www.reuters.com/article/us-health-youth-transgender/using-transgender-youths-chosen-names-may-lower-suicide-risk-idUSKBN1HH2WH.

11. "Facts about Suicide," Trevor Project, July 16, 2021, https://www.thetrevorproject.org/resources/preventing-suicide/facts-about-suicide/.

12. "Suicide Facts," Suicide Awareness Voices of Education, accessed August 31, 2021, https://save.org/about-suicide/suicide-facts/.

13. "Suicide Facts."

14. Devin Dwyer, "Transgender Student Wins Bathroom Battle after Supreme Court Rejects School Board Appeal," ABC News, June 28, 2021, https://abcnews.go.com/Politics/transgender-student-wins-bathroom-battle-supreme-court-rejects/story?id=78534829.

15. "State Equality Index 2020," Human Rights Campaign, last modified March 22, 2021, https://www.hrc.org/resources/state-equality-index.

16. Ruby Sales, "Spiritual Meaning of the Signs of the Times," interview by Jeff Clark, Wild Goose Festival, Hot Springs, NC, July 13, 2018.

## Chapter 3: So That All Means All

1. Bishop Tonia Rawls (lecture at MPOLIS Conference sponsored by Repairers of the Breach, Whitakers, NC, October 30, 2015).

2. *Ted Lasso*, season 1, episode 8, "The Diamond Dogs," directed by Declan Lowney, released September 18, 2020, on Apple TV+.

3. Sarah Moon and Hollie Silverman, "A California Fire Sparked by a Gender Reveal Party Has Grown to More Than 10,000 Acres," CNN, September 8, 2020, https://www.cnn.com/2020/09/08/us/el-dorado-fire-gender-reveal-update-trnd/index.html.

4. Mark Sameth, "Is God Transgender?," *New York Times*, August 12, 2016, https://www.nytimes.com/2016/08/13/opinion/is-god-transgender.html.

5. Tamara Ikenberg, "Television: The Rev. Jerry Falwell Insists the Purple Baby-Show Character Tinky Winky Is Homosexual," *Baltimore Sun*, February 11, 1999, https://www.baltimoresun.com/news/bs-xpm-1999-02-11-9902110274-story.html.

6. Tim Fitzsimons, "LGBTQ Political Representation Jumped 21 Percent in Past Year, Data Shows," MSNBC, July 16, 2020, https://www.nbcnews.com/feature/nbc-out/lgbtq-political-representation-jumped-21-percent-past-year-data-shows-n1234045.

7. Fitzsimons.

8. "Lesbian, Gay, Bisexual, and Transgender Workplace Issues (Quick Take)," *Catalyst*, June 1, 2021, https://www.catalyst.org/research/lesbian-gay-bisexual-and-transgender-workplace-issues/.

9. Jennica Webster, "Examining the Impact of LGBT Senior Leadership Representation on Business Outcomes: 2018 Wisconsin LGBT Chamber of Commerce Survey Feedback Report," August 6, 2018, https://wislgbtchamber.com/wp-content/uploads/2018/08/WI-LGBT-Chamber-Impact-of-LGBT-Leadership-on-Business-Outcomes-Report.pdf.

10. *Friends*, season 7, episode 6, "The One with the Nap Partners," directed by Gary Halvorson, aired November 9, 2000, on NBC.

11. *The Office*, season 3, episode 1, "Gay Witch Hunt," directed by Ken Kwapis, aired September 21, 2006, on NBC.

## Gay, White, and Male

1. Brené Brown, *Daring Greatly: How the Courage to Be Vulnerable Transforms the Way We Live, Love, Parent, and Lead* (New York: Avery, 2015), 47–53.

## Chapter 4: White Supremacy and the Air We Breathe

1. Robin DiAngelo, *White Fragility: Why It's So Hard for White People to Talk about Racism* (Boston: Beacon Press, 2018), 108.

2. DiAngelo, 22.

3. Martin Luther King Jr., "Letter from Birmingham Jail," in *A Testament of Hope: The Essential Writings and Speeches of Martin Luther King, Jr.*, ed. James M. Washington (San Francisco: HarperSanFrancisco, 1991), 296.

4. Kelly M. Hoffman et al., "Racial Bias in Pain Assessment and Treatment Recommendations, and False Beliefs about Biological Differences between Blacks and Whites," *Proceedings of the National Academy of Sciences of the United States of America* 113, no. 16 (2016): 4296–301, cited in DiAngelo, *White Fragility*, 63.

5. DiAngelo, *White Fragility*, 85.

6. Eduardo Bonilla-Silva, *Racism without Racists: Color-Blind Racism and the Persistence of Racial Inequality in America,* 6th ed. (Lanham, MA: Rowman and Littlefield, 2021).

7. James Baldwin, "A Conversation with James Baldwin," interview by Kenneth Clark, June 24, 1963, GBH Archives, http://openvault.wgbh.org/catalog/V_C03ED1927DCF46B5A8C82275DF4239F9.

8. James Baldwin, *The Fire Next Time* (New York: Vintage International, 1963), 22.

9. Resmaa Menakem, *My Grandmother's Hands: Racialized Trauma and the Pathway to Mending Our Hearts and Bodies* (Las Vegas, NV: Central Recovery Press, 2017), 60.

10. Nell Irvin Painter, *The History of White People* (New York: W. W. Norton, 2010), 193.

11. Painter, 193.

12. Max Weber, "The Religion of Non-Privileged Strata," in *Economy and Society,* ed. Guenther Roth and Claus Wittich (Berkeley: University of California Press, 1978), 490–91.

13. "Fatal Violence against the Transgender and Gender Non-Conforming Community in 2021," Human Rights Campaign, accessed August 27, 2021, https://www.hrc.org/resources/fatal-violence-against-the-transgender-and-gender non-conforming-community-in-2021.

14. Ta-Nehisi Coates, "The Case for Reparations," *Atlantic,* June 2014, https://www.theatlantic.com/magazine/archive/2014/06/the-case-for-reparations/361631/.

15. Coates.

16. Coates.

17. Coates.

18. Judith Carney, "The African Origins of Carolina Rice Culture," *Ecumene* 7, no. 2 (April 2000): 125–49, http://www.jstor.org/stable/44252124.

19. Betty Joyce Nash, "Rice to Riches," *Region Focus,* Winter 2008, 36–38, https://www.richmondfed.org/publications/research/econ_focus/2008/winter/~/media/C1F64F7DD7454FC9830627B3E986B37D.ashx.

20. Carney, "Carolina Rice Culture."

21. Coates, "Case for Reparations."

22. Coates.

23. Timothy B. Tyson, *Blood Done Sign My Name: A True Story* (New York: Crown Publishers, 2004), 272.

24. Tyson, 273.

25. Painter, *History of White People,* 110.

26. Painter, 113.

27. Painter, 118.

28. DiAngelo, *White Fragility,* 67.

## Chapter 5: Shedding Whiteness

1. Naomi Tutu, ed., *The Words of Desmond Tutu* (New York: Newmarket Press, 1996), 30.

2. Martin Luther King Jr., "Letter from Birmingham Jail," in *A Testament of Hope: The Essential Writings and Speeches of Martin Luther King, Jr.,* ed. James M. Washington (San Francisco: HarperSanFrancisco, 1991), 295.

3. Austin Channing Brown, *I'm Still Here: Black Dignity in a World Made for Whiteness* (New York: Convergent Books, 2018), 171.

4. Ruby Sales, "Where Does It Hurt?," interview with Krista Tippett, *On Being with Krista Tippett,* September 15, 2016, https://onbeing.org/programs/ruby-sales-where-does-it-hurt/.

5. James Baldwin, *The Fire Next Time* (New York: Vintage International, 1963), 98.

6. Brown, *I'm Still Here,* 88.

7. Jonathan Wilson-Hartgrove, *Reconstructing the Gospel: Finding Freedom from Slaveholder Religion* (Downers Grove, IL: InterVarsity Press, 2018), 164.

8. Brown, *I'm Still Here,* 170.

9. Ta-Nehisi Coates, "The Case for Reparations," *Atlantic,* June 2014, https://www.theatlantic.com/magazine/archive/2014/06/the-case-for-reparations/361631/.

10. Amy Roeder, "America Is Failing Its Black Mothers," *Harvard Public Health,* Winter 2019, https://www.hsph.harvard.edu/magazine/magazine_article/america-is-failing-its-Black-mothers/.

11. Sales, "Where Does It Hurt?"

12. Ta-Nehisi Coates, *Between the World and Me* (New York: Spiegel & Grau, 2015), 7.

13. Martin Luther King Jr., "Three Dimensions of a Complete Life" (sermon delivered at New Covenant Baptist Church in Chicago, April 9, 1967). Partial transcript available at https://special.seattletimes.com/o/special/mlk/king/completelife.html.

## Chapter 6: Patriarchy's Toxic Fruit

1. bell hooks, *The Will to Change: Men, Masculinity, and Love* (New York: Washington Square Press, 2004), 18.
2. Sarah Bessey, *Jesus Feminist: An Invitation to Revisit the Bible's View of Women* (New York: Howard Books, 2013), 78.
3. Erin Wathen, *Resist and Persist: Faith and the Fight for Equality* (Louisville, KY: Westminster John Knox Press, 2018), 100.
4. Wathen, 100.
5. Jared Yates Sexton, *The Man They Wanted Me to Be: Toxic Masculinity and a Crisis of Our Own Making* (Berkeley, CA: Counterpoint, 2019), 70.
6. hooks, *Will to Change,* 154.
7. Sharon G. Smith et al., *National Intimate Partner and Sexual Violence Survey: 2015 Data Brief–Updated Release* (Atlanta: National Center for Injury Prevention and Control, Centers for Disease Control and Prevention, November 2018), https://www.cdc.gov/violence prevention/pdf/2015data-brief508.pdf.
8. Wathen, *Resist and Persist,* 138.
9. Wathen, 111.
10. Wathen, 111.

## Chapter 7: Detoxifying Masculinity

1. Erin Wathen, *Resist and Persist: Faith and the Fight for Equality* (Louisville, KY: Westminster John Knox Press, 2018), 112.
2. Fred Craddock, *Craddock Stories,* ed. Mike Graves and Richard F. Ward (St. Louis: Chalice Press, 2001), 48–49.
3. Abraham Joshua Heschel, *Moral Grandeur and Spiritual Audacity: Essays,* ed. Susannah Heschel (New York: Noonday Press, 1996), viii–ix.
4. Lisa Davison, "Just Language Covenant," quoted in Wathen, *Resist and Persist,* 55.

## Chapter 8: Know Better, Do Better

1. Jonathan Wilson-Hartgrove, *Reconstructing the Gospel: Finding Freedom from Slaveholder Religion* (Downers Grove, IL: InterVarsity Press, 2018), 102.

2. Raj Nadella, "Seeking Justice in an Inherently Flawed System (John 5:1–9)," *HuffPost,* updated April 26, 2017, https://www .huffpost.com/entry/seeking-wholeness-in-an-inherently-flawed-system -john-51-9-by-dr-raj-nadella_b_9773900.

3. Deut. 6:10–11.

4. Rom. 8:31–39.

5. Stanley Hauerwas and William H. Willimon, *Resident Aliens: A Provocative Christian Assessment of Culture and Ministry for People Who Know That Something Is Wrong* (Nashville: Abingdon Press, 1989).

6. Hauerwas and Willimon, 12.

7. Hauerwas and Willimon, 125.

CPSIA information can be obtained
at www.ICGtesting.com
Printed in the USA
LVHW030758240322
714027LV00003B/6